BRIDGEWAYS

Group Style 3

English Conversation

-Learning English Has Never Been So Easy-

HAKMUNSA.com

머리말

학생들이 영어회화 시간에 대화 학습 활동을 할 때에는 4~5명 단위의 소그룹으로 편성하는 것이 효과적입니다. 영어회화를 가르치는 교사는 학생들이 교실에서의 대화 진행 활동에 적극적으로 참여하지 않는다고 신경을 쓰며 걱정 할 것은 못됩니다.
학생들이 골고루 돌아가며 대화에 참여할 수 있는 균등한 기회가 주어 질수 있도록 대화 진행 분위기를 조성해 주는 것이 무엇보다 중요합니다.
소그룹 편성시 유의할 점은 우선 학생들이 서로 편안하게 느끼는 대화상대 3~4명씩 서로 선택할 수 있도록 하여 학생들의 대화 참여 기회를 증가시켜 주게 해야 합니다.
또 그룹 중의 한명은 보다 능력 있는 학생 1명씩 반드시 배정하여 주는 것도 중요한 진행 방침입니다.
왜냐하면 그렇게 함으로써 다른 학생들은 좀더 능력 있는 자로부터 배울 수 있으며 보다 진전된 회화를 할 수 있어 학생들이 실제로 대화 기회를 적극적으로 증가 시켜 줍니다.
이렇게 해서 더 미숙한 학생들이 좀 더 능력 있는 이들로부터 배울 수 있는 가능성을 높이고 그룹원들이 좀 더 조화롭게 어울릴 수 있는 분위기를 조성할 수 있게 됩니다.

게다가 이책은 원어민의 "일상언어" 습득에도 참여할 수 있는 기회를 배려하고 있습니다.
"일상생활언어"란 원어민들이 일상 생활에서 편안하게 사용하는 생활언어입니다. 우리 학생들은 영어 수업상의 교실영어 뿐만 아니라 실제 삶에서 사용되는 언어도 또한 배울수 있게 되어 해외여행에서 현지민의 일상생활을 더 잘 익힐 수 있도록 하게 될 것입니다.

First published 2008
HAKMUNSA.com
37-18 haengchon-dong Jongno-gu Seoul, korea
Tel 02-738-5118 Fax 02-725-8023
http://www.hakmun.co.kr

Price : ₩8,500

ISBN 978-89-5647-008-5
ISBN 978-89-5647-009-2(전3권)

BRIDGEWAYS

Group Style

3

Paul Z. Jambor

English Conversation

- Learning English Has Never Been So Easy -

HAKMUN PUBLISHING CO.

Author: **Paul Z. Jambor**

An EFL Book for Korean Learners of English

Bridgeways 3

Group Styled English Conversation

Learning English Has Never Been So Easy

Never has it been so easy to learn English conversation. It only takes a group of learners to utilize this book to get maximum results. That is to say, conversation can only be learned if the language is applied in real use, and what better way to do this than to take part in group conversation in contexts outlined by this book.

First published 2008

Seoul, Korea

http://www.hakmun.co.kr

Price: ₩13,000

ISBN: 978-89-467-8336-2

Foreword

It is important that students form small groups of 4-5 students as they facilitate conversation in the English Classroom. Teachers of English as a foreign language often complain that learners do not engage in oral conversational activities within their classrooms. What they may not realize is that it is often very challenging for learners to do so if the classroom is not set up so as to give the learners the opportunity to converse. It is best to place at least one 'more capable' learner within the group since it gives the other learners the opportunity to improve their conversational abilities. Also, it is a good idea to have learners choose their own groups in order to give them the chance to choose group members they feel most comfortable with. This dramatically increases the chances that learners will actually converse. Perhaps the best method is to pick the more capable learners ahead of time so they can pick 3-4 members they feel most at ease with. This increases the chances for group harmony and the likelihood that the weaker learners will learn from the more capable others.

What is more, this book exposes learners to some instances of 'casual language'. In essence, 'casual language' is language native speakers use in everyday situations. This allows learners to learn not only the English of the English class, but

Table of Contents

Unit	Topics	Pages
Unit 1 The world of Friends	• Greetings and Introductions • Exchanging Personal Information • Saying goodbye • Asking for personal data • Talking about personal interests • Exchanging Personal Identity Information	p.8 - Introductions and Greetings p.9 - Asking Personal Questions p.10 - Parting/Leave-taking & Personal Interests p.11 - Personal Identity and Personal Data p.12 - Making Conversation in Real Context p.13 - Review Activities: Writing in Context p.14 - Puzzle
Unit 2 My Daily Schedule	• Expressing future tense with the present continuous • Expressing general routines with the present continuous • Enquiring about daily routines • Making General Enquiries • Making Future Enquiries	p.16 - Other People's Plans p.17 - Daily Routines p.18 - Acknowledgements p.19 - General and Future Tense Enquiries p.20 - Present Continuous for Future Tense p.21 - Review Activities p.22 - Puzzle
Unit 3 Earning a Living	• Asking "Why?" questions • Ways of prolonging and sustaining conversations • How to express abstract concepts about work and school • Likes and dislikes toward certain jobs	p.24 - Future Dreams p.25 - Job Specifics p.26 - Sustaining Conversations p.27 - Is your Job Interesting? p.28 - Active Listening p.29 - Review Activity p.30 - Puzzle
Unit 4 Simple Cooking	• The Varieties of Home Prepared Cuisines • Making Dinner Invitations • Using Adjectives to Describe Foods • Agreeing with Others	p.32 - What are you …? p.33 - Complementing Others p.34 - Showing Agreement p.35 - Making Dinner Plans p.36 - Active Listening p.37 - Review Activity p.38 - Puzzle
Unit 5 Cash for a Living	• Banking Terminologies • Making Withdrawals • Using and ATM • Transferring Money • Using Debit Cards	p.40 - Breaking Bills & Shopping p.41 - Paying Bills and Withdrawing p.42 - Banking Terminologies p.43 - Using an ATM p.44 - Comprehension Activities p.45 - Review Activities p.46 - Puzzle

Unit	Topics	Pages
Unit 6 **Public Transportation**	• The different modes of transportation • Getting around using public transportation • Transportation Terminology • Asking people how to get to places.	p.48 - Comparative Adjectives p.49 - Comprehension Activities p.50 - Taking the Train p.51 - Transportation Terminology p.52 - Listening Comprehension p.53 - Review Activities p.54 - Puzzle
Unit 7 **Computers in Daily Life**	• Computer Terminology • Providing and asking for assistance in using a computer • Using a computer and other peripheral devices • The type of activities and jobs computers are used for	p.56 - Printing Documents p.57 - Clicking and Saving p.58 - Computer Terminology p.59 - Adjusting the Monitor p.60 - Comprehension Activities p.61 - Review Activities p.62 - Puzzle
Unit 8 **Music Is My Life**	• Music Terminology • Music Genres • Musical Instruments • Conversation about Concert Venues • Selecting the right music	p.64 - Playing Music and Instruments p.65 - Live Music and Concerts p.66 - Music Terminology p.67 - Music Genres and Selections p.68 - Comprehension Activities p.69 - Review Activities p.70 - Puzzle
Unit 9 **Sports & Leisure**	• Recreation related terms • Having conversations about recreational activities • Useful idiomatic expressions • Expressing likes and dislikes using adjectives	p.72 - In The Swimming Pool p.73 - Sailing is Amazing p.74 - Idiomatic Expressions p.75 - Snorkelling Fun p.76 - Comprehension Activities p.77 - Review Activities p.78 - Puzzle
Unit 10 **Into the Future**	• The varieties of Future Tense • Future Conditionals • Conversations about future events • Future Tense Conversations	p.80 - At the hair salon p.81 - I'll be a truck driver p.82 - Future Conditionals p.83 - I'm going shopping p.84 - Comprehension Activities p.85 - Review Activities p.86 - Puzzle

Unit 11 **Long, Long Ago**	• The Present Perfect Simple and The Present Perfect Progressive • How to talk about things that have existed a long time • Talking about the distant past • Past Tense Interrogative	p.88 - Present Perfect Simple p.89 - Present Perfect Progressive p.90 - Past Tenses p.91 - When I was a boy p.92 - Comprehension Activities p.93 - Review Activities p.94 - Puzzle
Unit 12 **Fashion and Trends**	• Fashion Terms • The Modal Verb 'Should' • Making a selection • Picking the right size	p.96 - Footwear p.97 - Making a Selection p.98 - Fashion Terms p.99 - For the Right Occasion p.100 - Comprehension Activities p.101 - Review Activities p.102 - Puzzle
Hidden Tape Scripts	• Transcripts of conversations (Activity 11:b -T5) in each of the respective units	p.103
Puzzle Solutions	• Solutions to the puzzles at the end of each respective unit	p.110
Complementary Activities	• Additional activities that correlate to activities within the respective units	p.114
Supplementary Materials	• Supplementary materials that correlate to activities within the respective units	p.115
Irregular Verbs	• A list of irregular verbs and their past tenses	p.116
Guide to Using Bridgeways	**IMPORTANT!** • This section is required reading before learners start on Unit 1	p.118
Attention Teachers!	**IMPORTANT!** • All teachers should read this section before they start any lessons	p.121

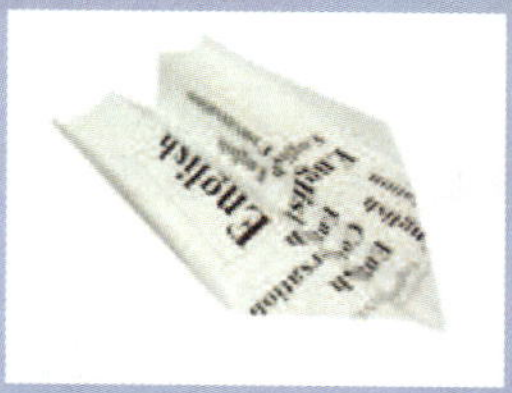

BUSINESS NAME

Unit 1

The World of Friends

It's a pleasure to meet you. *The pleasure is all mine.*

Grammar Content

- Simple Present
- Interrogative
- The Noun Phrase
- Singular

Unit breakdown:

Introductions & Greetings p. 8

Personal Questions p. 9

Leave-taking & Personal Interests p. 10

Personal Identity p. 11

Conversing in Real Context p. 12

Review Activities p. 13

Puzzle p. 14

New and Old Friends

This unit focuses on …

- Greetings and introductions
- Exchanging personal information
- Saying goodbye
- Asking for personal data
- Talking about personal interests
- Exchanging personal identity information

Hi.

Hello there

1) Please allow me to introduce myself.

A) Hi, there.
B) Hello.

A) I am David Cooper.
B) Cathy Moore.

A) Hi, Cathy. It's a pleasure to meet you.
B) The pleasure is all mine.

A) I'd like to give you my business card.
B) Sure! Thanks.

I would like to = I'd like to

Now practice the above conversation within your group. Use your own names while making up your own scenarios and say them out loud in English. Don't forget to involve all group members.

2) Introducing Others

"I'd like to meet your friend. Could you introduce her to me?"

A) Hi, Josh.
B) What's up, John?
A) Hey Josh! Could you introduce me to your friend?
B) -Ok. Come on.
-Hi, Jennifer.
C) Hi, Josh. How's it going?
B) Good. How are you?
C) Not bad.
B) Jennifer, this is my friend, John from school.
C) Hi, John. It's nice to meet you.
A) The pleasure is all mine.
C) So, are you from around here?
A) No. I'm from New York.
C) New York? Well, you're a city boy.
A) Yes, I am. But I've been living here two years now.
C) Well, I sure hope to see you around.
A) Yes. Me, too.

Now practice the above conversation within your group. Use your own names while making up your own scenarios and say them out loud in English. Don't forget to involve all group members.

3) Personal Interests T1

- So! What do you like doing in your free time?
- I like making new friends.
- Where do you usually meet new people?
- I usually go to the sea to meet new friends. The beach is a good place to chat.

4) Introducing Other People T2

A) Mark. I'd like to introduce you to my friend Danielle.

Mark, this is Danielle. - Danielle, this is Mark.

B) Hi Danielle. It's good to meet you.

C) Good to meet you, too, Mark.

B) Are you here for pleasure or business?

C) Pleasure, of course. I am here every weekend.

B) Really? It is wonderful here though, isn't it? I sure would like to spend more time here, too.

C) I don't see why not. The beach is only one hour away from the city. You can even take the train.

B) That's true. But I am usually busy on the weekends. I am a chef at the Grand Hotel.

C) Oh, good for you.

Now practice the above conversation within your group. Use your own names while making up your own scenarios and say them out loud in English. Don't forget to involve all group members.

5) Comprehension Activity

	True	False
1) Danielle is at the beach for business.	☐	☐
2) Mark goes to the beach every weekend.	☐	☐
3) Mark can't take a train to the beach.	☐	☐
4) Danielle is a chef at the Grand Hotel.	☐	☐
5) The beach is far from the city.	☐	☐
6) Mark doesn't want to spend much time at the beach.	☐	☐
7) Mark is usually busy on the weekends.	☐	☐

6) On the Weekends

Q What do you prefer doing on the weekends?

A I like spending time with my friends.
My friends are really wonderful people.

Q Do you have any plans for the weekend?

A Not really. I am planning on staying home and doing nothing. Just relaxing really.

Now practice the above conversation within your group. Use your own scenarios and say them out loud in English. Don't forget to involve all group members.

7) Greetings and Leave-taking

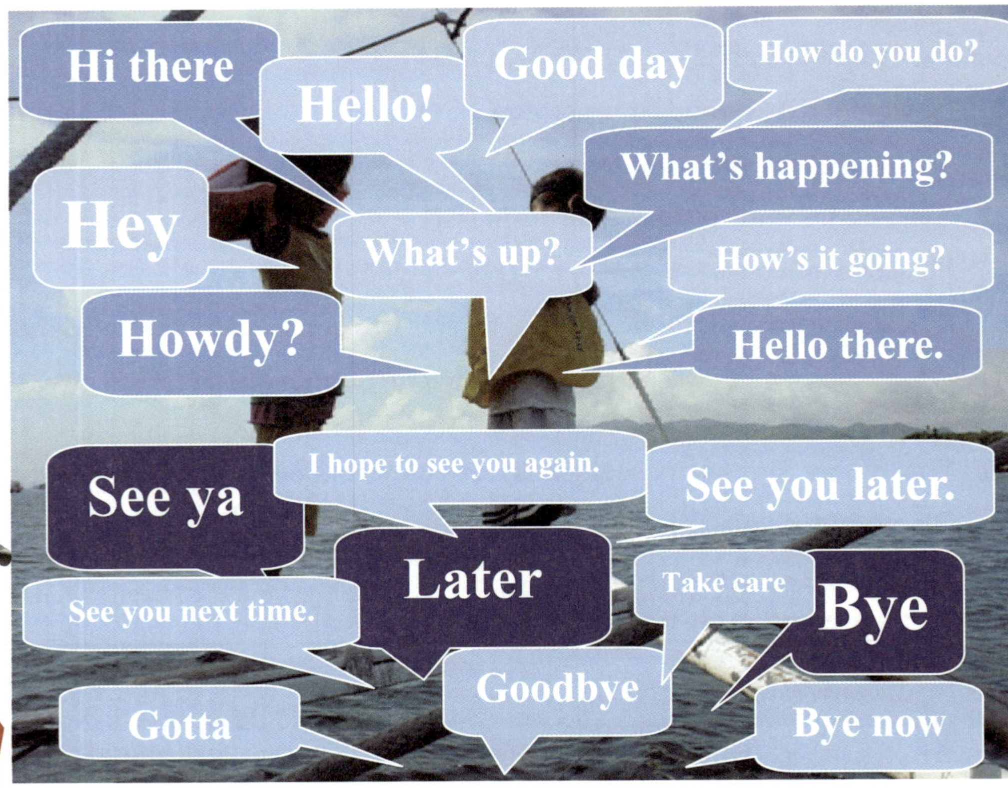

Howdy? = How do you do? have got to = gotta

Now practice the above illustrated ways of greeting and leave-taking. It is important that you know how to use and understand all of them. Don't forget to involve all group members.

8: a) What do you like to do in your free time? 🎧 T3

A) What do you like doing in your free time, Jeff?

B) I like to go to the sea on the weekends.

A) Really? What do you usually do there?

B) I like snorkeling and swimming with the fish.

A) That sounds really interesting.

B) I also enjoy going sailing with friends.

A) No kidding? Wow! It sounds like going to the sea is very exciting.

B) It most certainly is.

A) Perhaps, next time we can go together. What do you think?

B) I don't know. I'll have to think about that.

Now practice the above conversation within your group. Use your own names while making up your own scenarios and say them out loud in English. Don't forget to involve all group members.

8: b) Personal Identity T4

A) May I have your name please?

B) Yes. My name is Michael Washington.

A) OK. Could you give me your address please?

B) 65 Maple street, Ottawa, Ontario.

A) Could you also give me your postal code please?

B) M5T-2R7

A) And now for your birthday.

B) May 6th, 1983.

A) Good. Where were you born?

B) In Toronto.

A) Great. Thank you very much.

Name: Michael B. Washington
Gender: Male
Address: 65 Maple st.
Ottawa, Ontario
M5T-2R7
Birthday: May 6, 1983
Place of Birth: Toronto

ID Number: B-1234987-HJ89

Now ask your group members for their personal information. Use the conversation in activity 8 as a model for your conversations.

9) Do you have an ID card?

A) May I ask who you are?

B) Sure. I'm Peter Black.

A) Do you have an ID card?

B) Will a driver's license do?

A) Yes, a driver's license is just fine.

B) Here you are.

A) Thank you.
So, you're from Vancouver.

B) Yes. That's right.

Name: Peter J. Black
Gender: Male
Address: 1254 Base Road
Vancouver, British
Columbia
B7G-4Y8
Birthday: June 23, 1976
Place of Birth: Vancouver

ID Number: A-4321789-BV98

"May I please have your personal information?"

Now take the given conversation and model your own conversations on it. Once again use your own information.

10) Fill in the missing information

Name: ____________
Gender: ____
Address: ____________
____
____
____
Birthday: ________
Place of Birth: ________

ID Number:

Name: ____________
Gender: ____
Address: ____________
____
____
____
Birthday: ________
Place of Birth: ________

ID Number:

Now take turns filling in the missing information on the ID cards. Create assumed identities and give your group members your personal data.

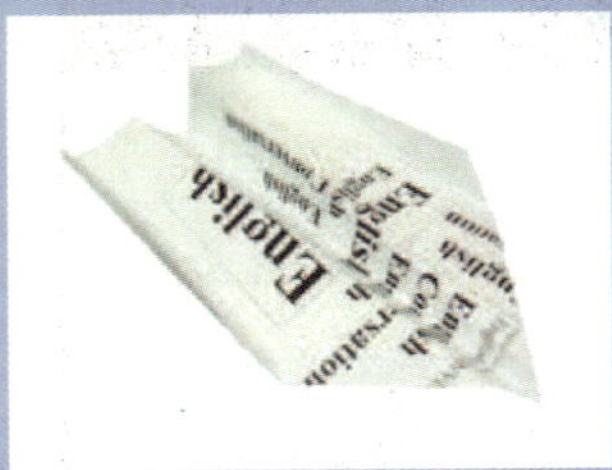

What is your passion?

11: a) Fill in the missing information

Fill in the missing information by asking your group members for their information..

	Example	Friend 1	Friend 2	Friend 3
Name	Peter			
Interests	Hiking and Dancing			
Goals	Doctor or CEO			
Desires	Good Husband & Father			
Passion ♥♥♥	Playing the Guitar			

A) What is your passion Peter?
B) My passion is to (verb + noun/noun phrase). [My passion is to travel the world.]

A) What are your interests?
B) I enjoy (verb + noun/noun phrase). [I enjoy going hiking and dancing.]

A) What are your goals?
B) I hope to (verb + noun/noun phrase). [I hope to become a doctor or to be the CEO of a multinational company.]

A) What are your desires?
B) I'd like to (verb + noun/noun phrase). [I'd like to have a wonderful husband/wife and two lovely little children.]

11: b) Listening Comprehension T5

Fill in the missing information by listening to the conversations.

	Jennifer	Michael
What are her/his interests?		
What are her/his passions?		
What are her/his goals?		

12: a) Write your own conversation (Introductions)

Write a conversation wherein you introduce two friends to one another. A) is you, while B) & C) are your friends.

A) ______________________________

B) ______________________________

A) ______________________________

B) ______________________________

C) ______________________________

B) ______________________________

C) ______________________________

B) ______________________________

C) ______________________________

Now practice the conversations with your group. Remember to involve all group members.

12: b) Write your own conversation (Personal Interests)

Write a conversation wherein you ask someone about their interests, desires, goals and passions.

A) ______________________________

B) ______________________________

A) ______________________________

B) ______________________________

A) ______________________________

B) ______________________________

A) ______________________________

"What do you usually do when you're not working/ studying?"

12: c) Your own free time

Write about what you like doing in your own free time.

____

____

____

____

____

____

____

13) Puzzle

Use the sentences found in Unit 1 to help you complete the following puzzle.

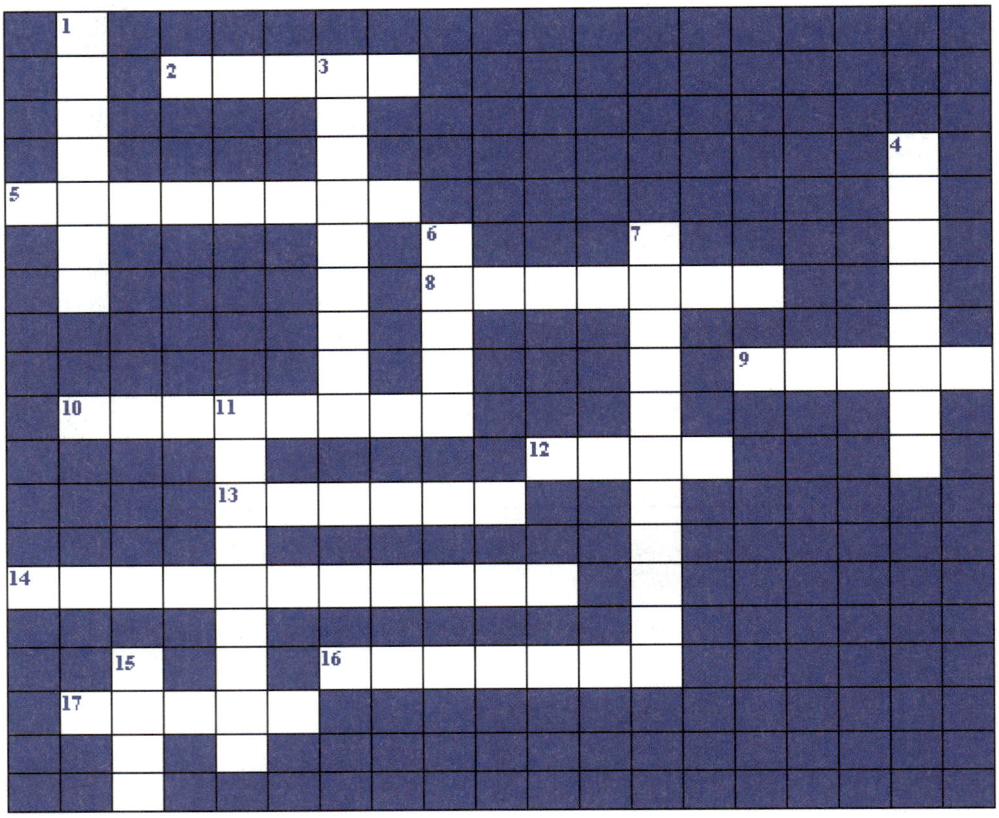

After you have completed the puzzle, check the 'Puzzle Solutions' section at the back of the book for the solution to the above puzzle.

Across

2) You can take the ______ to the beach.
5) It's a __________ to meet you.
8) Will a driver's __________ do?
9) How's it __________?
10) Are you here for pleasure or __________?
12) What do you usually do in your free _______?
13) Your ________ code please.
14) That sounds ____________.
16) My __________ is to travel the world.
17) I'll have to __________ about that.

Down

1) Where do you __________ meet new people?
3) Could you __________ her to me?
4) I am usually busy on the _____________.
6) Do you have any _________ for the weekend?
7) May I please have your personal ___________?
11) Friends are very ____________ to me.
15) The beach is a good place to ________.

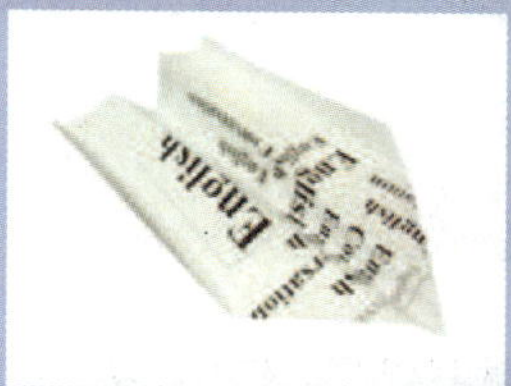

BUSINESS NAME

Unit 2

My Daily Schedule

Daily Routines

Grammar Content

- Present Continuous and its use to express future events

Unit breakdown:

Other People's Plans	p. 16
Daily Routines	p. 17
Acknowledge-ment	p. 18
General & Future Tense Enquiries	p. 19
Present Continuous for Future	p. 20
Review Activities	p. 21
Puzzle	p. 22

My Daily Routine

This unit focuses on …

- Expressing future tense with the present continuous
- Expressing general routines with the present continuous
- Enquiring about daily routines
- Making general enquiries
- Making future enquiries

OK

Not much.

1) What are you doing today?

A) Do you have any special plans for today?

B) No, not at all.

A) Are you staying home alone?

B) Yes, I think so. I enjoy being by myself.

A) Are you going to order in?

B) No, I am having some spicy Korean instant noodle soup.

A) Well, enjoy your time alone.

B) OK. Bye bye.

Now practice the above conversation within your group. Use your own scenarios and say them out loud in English.

Verb + (ing) can be used to express future events

2) Are you doing anything special today?

A) Are you doing anything special today?

B) Yes, I am meeting my mother for lunch.

A) Are you eating out?

B) Yes, we are.

A) Where are you meeting?

B) We're meeting at McDonalds.

A) What are you having?

B) Probably Big Macs.

A) What are you doing after lunch?

B) Nothing special.

A) Do you want to go to the movies later tonight then?

B) Sure. That sounds good.

A) Where should we meet?

B) Let's meet at the Sports Café.

let us = let's

Now practice the above conversation within your group. Use your own scenarios and say them out loud in English. Don't forget to involve all group members.

---

3) Listen to The Conversation T1

- Are you going to be at school tomorrow morning?
- Yes, of course.
- What time will you be arriving?
- I am arriving at 7:50 am. Just before class starts.

4) What do you do during the week? T2

Peter) What do you usually do during the week?
Lydia) I usually go out to town to buy some necessities.
Peter) What kind of things do you buy?
Lydia) Nothing special, really. Just the basic staples.
Peter) Staples?
Lydia) Yes! You know. Things like bread, milk, meat, vegetables, flour and water.
The basic necessities.
Peter) Oh! I see.
Lydia) Do you need anything?
Peter) No, thank you. I am fine.

Now practice the above conversation within your group. Use your own scenarios and say them out loud in English.

---

5) Comprehension Activity

		True	False
1)	Peter usually buys staples on weekdays.	□	□
2)	Lydia usually goes out to town on weekdays.	□	□
3)	Lydia usually buys staples for her stapler.	□	□
4)	Candy is a basic staple.	□	□
5)	Peter doesn't need anything.	□	□
6)	Lydia only buys milk on weekdays.	□	□

---

6) Are you going shopping?

Q Are you going shopping today?
A Yes, I am. I need to buy some clothes for the summer.

Q Are you buying a skirt for the warm weather?
A No. I'm buying a pair of shorts.

Now practice the above conversation within your group. Use your own scenarios and say them out loud in English.

7) Acknowledgements

The first group of acknowledgements is formal while the second group is less formal.

Now practice the above illustrated ways of acknowledging. It is important that you know how to use and understand all of them.

8: a) I'm glad to hear that. T3

Teacher) **My homework is not finished.**
Student) **I'm sorry to hear that.**

Friend 1) **I've brought you the book you asked for.**
Friend 2) **That's awesome.**

Colleague 1) **I finished the report you asked for.**
Colleague 2) **I am glad to hear that.**

Friend 1) **I can't meet you tonight. I have too much homework.**
Friend 2) **I see. Well, I'll see you tomorrow then.**

Now practice the above conversation within your group. Use your own scenarios and say them out loud in English.

8: b) General Enquiries T4

A) What do you do during the week?
B) I drive a bus for a living.
A) What are you doing in the evenings?
B) I play computer games and take out the trash.
A) What do you usually do in the mornings?
B) I feed the dog, take a shower and read the news.
A) What are you doing on the weekends?
B) I hike the trails near my mother's house.
A) Do you travel in your free time?
B) Yes, sometimes I do.

Now ask your group members about their daily routine. Use the conversation in activity 8 as a model for your conversations.

9) Future Tense Enquiries

A) What are you doing on the weekend?
B) I am playing basketball with my friends.

A) What are you doing at night?
B) I'm practicing English conversation.

A) What are you doing tomorrow morning?
B) I am driving to the airport.

A) What are you doing in an hour?
B) I am eating lunch.

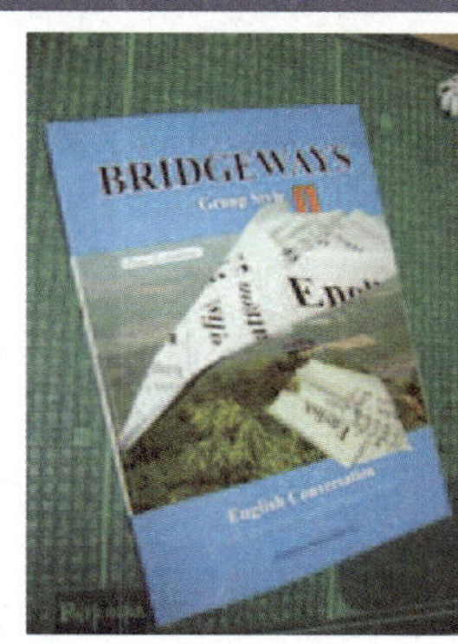

"What are you doing at 7:00 tonight?"

Now take the given conversation and model your own conversations on it. Use your own scenarios.

10) Complete The Charts (What do you usually do on ..?) (What are you doing ..?)

General Enquiries

	On Mondays	On Fridays
Student 1 ______		
Student 2 ______		

Future Enquiries

	This Evening	This Weekend
Student 1 ______		
Student 2 ______		

Now take turns filling in the missing information. Use your friends answers to complete the chart.

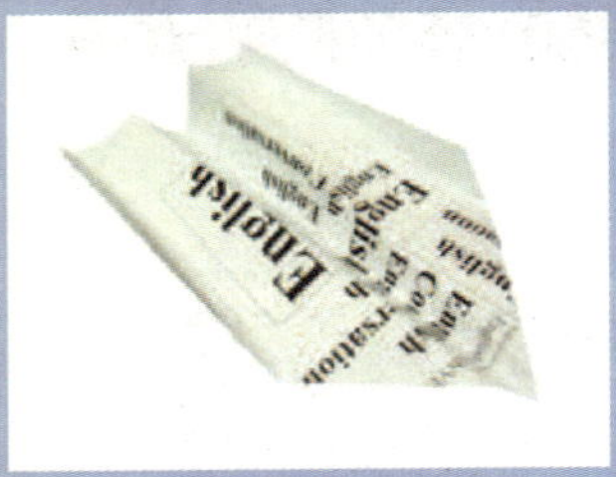

11: a) Fill in the missing information

Fill in the missing information by asking your group members some questions.

	Larry	Friend 1	Friend 2	Friend 3
On Weekdays	Studying English			
On the Weekends	Playing Cards			
Tonight	Watching TV			
Tomorrow Morning	Biking			
Next Week	Working			

A) What are you doing on weekdays Larry?
B) I study English. I am studying for a TOEIC test.

A) Are you doing anything special on the weekends?
B) I usually play cards with my colleagues. We always play at my apartment.

A) What are you doing tonight?
B) I am watching television all night. I am too tired to do anything else.

A) What are you doing tomorrow morning?
B) I am going bicycling with my friend Jeff.

A) What are you doing tomorrow?
B) Tomorrow I am working all day long.

11: b) Listening Comprehension T5

Fill in the missing information by listening to the conversations.

	Jack	Monica
What does s/he do during the week?		
What does s/he do on the weekends?		
What does s/he do in the evenings?		

12: a) Write your own conversation (General Enquiries)

Write a conversation wherein you ask someone about what s/he is doing in general on any given occasion.

A)
B)
A)
B)
A)
B)
A)
B)

Now act out the conversations you wrote with your group members.

12: b) Write your own conversation (Future Enquiries)

Write a conversation wherein you ask someone about what s/he is doing sometime in the future.

A)
B)
A)
B)
A)
B)
A)
B)

"What are you doing this weekend?"

12: c) Your Daily Routine

Write about your daily routine.

13) Puzzle

Use the sentences found in Unit 2 to help you complete the following puzzle.

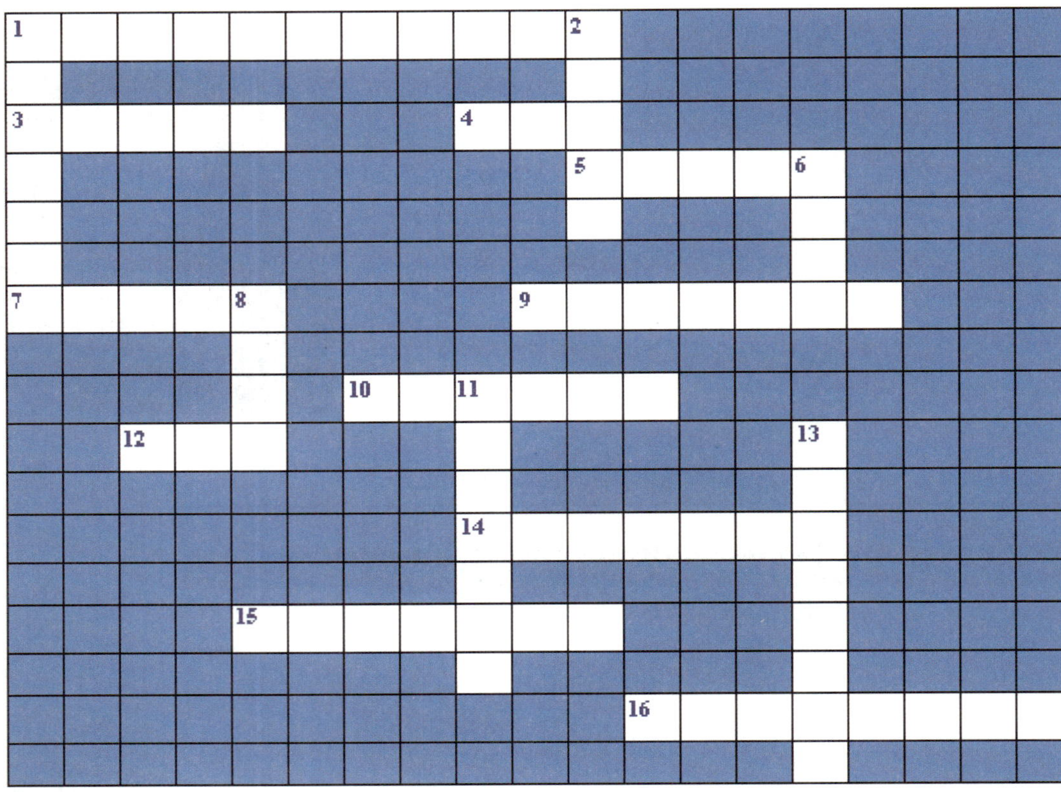

After you have completed the puzzle, check the 'Puzzle Solutions' section at the back of the book for the solution to the above puzzle.

Across

1) The basic _______________.
3) What are you doing ____________?
4) Good _______ you.
5) That's all __________.
7) Are you __________ shopping today?
9) ___________ are the basic necessities.
10) Yes, of ____________.
12) That's too ______.
14) That's _______________.
15) No ____________.
16) I'm ______________ English.

Down

1) ____________ special.
2) I'm _________ to hear that.
6) Do you travel in your free ________?
8) I'm ________ to hear that.
11) What do you _____________ do on weekdays?
13) What are you doing on the ______________?

Unit 3

Earning a Living

BUSINESS NAME

Grammar

Content

- Using the Conjunction 'When'
- Using the conjunction 'Because'
- The Modal Verb 'Should'

Unit breakdown:

Future Dreams p. 24

Job Specifics p. 25

Sustaining Conversations p. 26

Is Your Job Interesting? p. 27

Conversation Activities p. 28

Review Activities p. 29

Puzzle p. 30

Occupations

This unit focuses on …

- Asking "Why?" questions
- Ways of prolonging and sustaining conversations
- How to express abstract concepts about work and school
- Likes and dislikes toward certain jobs

Why?

Is that so?

1) Future Dreams

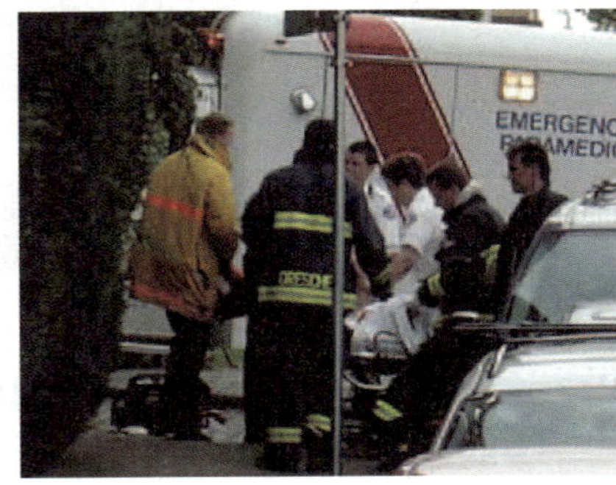

A) What's your future dream?
B) I'd like to be a paramedic.

A) Why?
B) Because the job is very exciting.

A) Is that so?
B) Yes, you get to save peoples' lives when they need emergency care.

A) So, you'd like it for sure.
B) Yes, of course.

you would like it = you'd like it

Now practice the above conversation within your group. Use your own scenarios and say them out loud in English. Don't forget to involve all group members.

"Good for you."

2) What would you like to do for a living?

A) What would you like to do for a living?

B) I'd like to be a hockey player.

A) Is playing hockey exciting?

B) Oh, yes. Scoring goals when the crowd is cheering is a lot of fun.

A) Do you score many goals?

B) Yes. I am the best player on my team.

A) Good for you.

Now practice the above conversation within your group. Use your own scenarios and say them out loud in English. Don't forget to involve all group members.

Listen to The Conversation T1

- What is your dream?
- To become the Prime Minister of Canada.
- Why?
- Because everyone respects the Prime Minister when they meet him.

4) Grammar in Context

Everyone	respects	the Prime Minister	when	they	meet him	.
You	get to save	peoples' lives		they	need emergency care	
I	like	being outside		it's	sunny	
My mother	is	happy		she	sings	

A) What is your future dream?
B) I'd like to be a coast guard.
A) Why?
B) People respect the coast guard when they save people's lives.

Now practice the above sentences within your group. Use your own ideas to construct your own sentences.

5) Listening Activity T2

A) How long does it take you to get to work?
B) I drive to work, so it only takes about 15 minutes.
A) The morning traffic is not too bad.
B) No, not at all. There are not many cars on the road.
A) I should drive, too.
B) Yes, you should.

6) Why not?

A) Do you like your job?
B) No, not really.
A) Why not? (Why don't you like it?)
B) Because I work outside, and it's too hot in the summer and very cold in the winter.
A) You should change your job then.
B) Yes, I should.

Now practice the above conversation within your group. Use your own scenarios to construct your own sentences.

7) Ways of Continuing Conversations

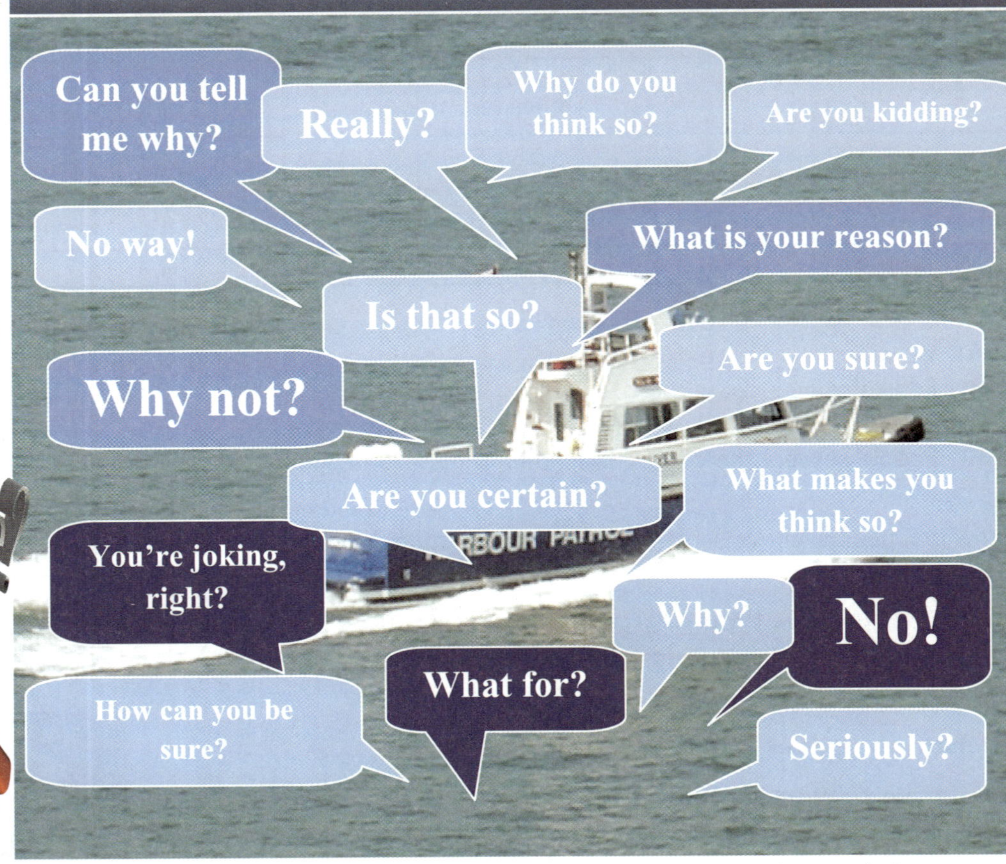

Now practice the above illustrated ways of continuing conversations. It is important that you know how to use and understand all of them. Don't forget to involve all group members.

8: a) Listening Activity 🎧 T3

A) Would you like to be a doctor?

B) No.

A) What is your reason?

B) Doctors have too much responsibility.

A) Is that so?

B) Yes. I'd rather be a horse carriage driver.

A) But, why?

B) Because the job is more or less stress free.

more or less = kind of = sort of

Now practice the above conversation within your group. Use your own scenarios and say them out loud in English. Don't forget to involve all group members.

8: b) Being a Policeman T4

A) What do you do for a living?

B) I'm a policeman.

A) What's the most interesting thing about your job?

B) Well, I think meeting different kinds of people is interesting.

A) Are you sure?

B) Yes, but I also think meeting new challenges is interesting, too.

A) I see.

Use the conversation in activity 8 as a model for your conversations.

9) You're a wonderful piano player.

A) You play the piano very well.

B) Thank you.

A) What is your secret?

B) Nothing really. Playing is very soothing. That's all.

A) I see.

"Playing the piano is very soothing. That's all."

Now take the given conversation and model your own conversations on it. Once again use your own scenarios.

10) What is the most interesting thing about being a student?

Example

Name: Benjamin Green

Why is it interesting being a student?

I like learning new information all the time.

Friend

Name: ____________

Why is it interesting being a student?

____

____

Now take turns filling in the missing information.

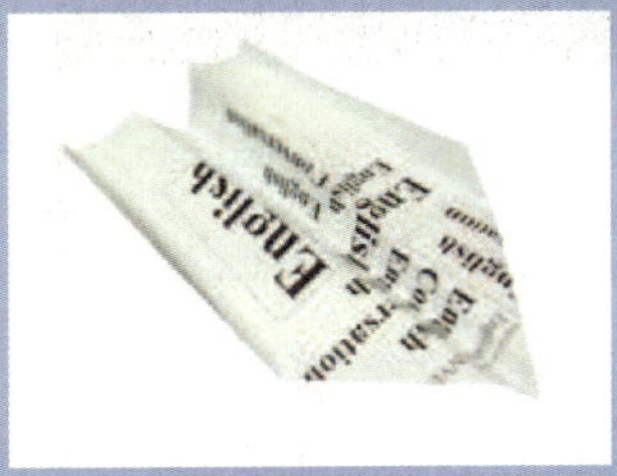

11: a) Fill in the missing information

Fill in the missing information by asking your group members some questions.

	Example	Friend 1	Friend 2
Name	James Cooper		
Why is your job/ course interesting?	I like learning new things.		
How long does it take to get to work/school?	It takes 35 minutes by bus.		
What would you like to do for a living?	I'd like to be a doctor.		
Why?	Doctors earn much money.		

A) Why is your course interesting?
B) Because I really like learning new things.

A) How long does it take to get to your school?
B) It takes about 35 minutes by bus.

A) What would you like to do for a living?
B) I'd like to be a doctor and work in a reputable hospital.

A) Why would you like to be a doctor?
B) Well, doctors earn a lot of money, and I love money.

11: b) Listening Comprehension T5

Fill in the missing information by listening to the conversations.

	Christina	Maria
Why is her job/ course interesting?		
How long does it take her to get to work/ school?		
How does she get to work/ school?		

12: a) Write your own conversation (Why?/Why not?)

Write a conversation wherein you ask someone why s/he likes her/his job/course.

A) ______________________________
B) ______________________________
A) ______________________________
B) ______________________________
A) ______________________________
B) ______________________________
A) ______________________________
B) ______________________________

Now act out the conversations you wrote with your group members. Remember to involve all group members.

12: b) Write your own conversation (General Enquiries)

Write a conversation wherein you ask someone random questions about their school job.

A) ______________________________
B) ______________________________
A) ______________________________
B) ______________________________
A) ______________________________
B) ______________________________
A) ______________________________
B) ______________________________

"How long does it take to get to your school?"

12: c) Free Writing

Write any conversation you can compose using information from this unit.

13) Puzzle

Use the sentences found in Unit 3 to help you complete the following puzzle.

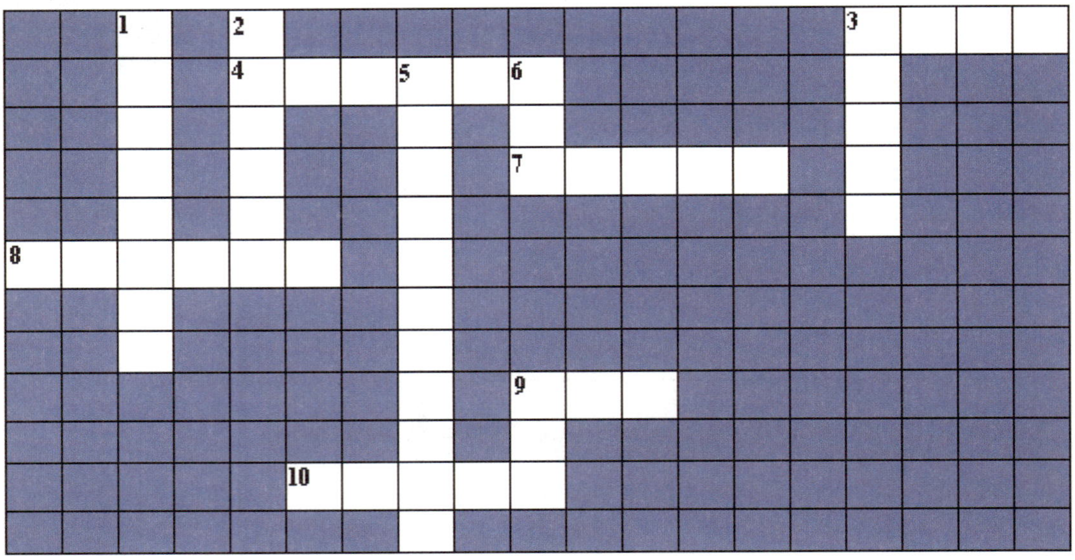

After you have completed the puzzle, check the 'Puzzle Solutions' section at the back of the book for the solution to the above puzzle.

Across

3) My mother is happy _______ she sings.
4) What would you like to do for a _________?
7) Why do you _________ so?
8) What's your __________ dream?
9) Can you tell me _______?
10) Doctors earn a lot of ________.

Down

1) My dream is to become the Prime __________ of Canada.
2) I am the best ________ on my team.
3) ________ you like to be a doctor?
5) Why is your course _____________?
6) How long does it take to ______ to work?
9) ______ would you like to be a teacher?

BUSINESS NAME

Unit 4
Simple Cooking

Grammar Content

- Adjectives
- Adverbs in use

Unit breakdown:

What are you …? p. 32

Complementing p. 33

Showing Agreement p. 34

Making Dinner Plans p. 35

Active Listening p. 36

Review Activities p. 37

Puzzle p. 38

Home Made Cuisines

This unit focuses on …

- The varieties of gome prepared cuisines
- Making invitations
- Using adjectives to describe foods
- Agreeing with others

Why not? As Soon As...

1) Would you like some sausages?

A) Would you like to eat some sausages?
B) Sure. Let's have some barbecued sausages.
A) That's a good idea. I'll start up the barbecue.
B) Are you going to barbecue the sausages here at home?
A) Sure, why not? There is a barbecue in the back yard.
B) Ok. Let's do it then.

Now practice the above conversation within your group. Use your own scenarios and say them out loud in English. Don't forget to involve all group members.

"All right. As soon as I cook them up."

2) What are you making?

A) What are you making?
B) I'm making some <u>home made sausages</u>.
A) Really? Are they any good?
B) They're really good you know.
A) Can I try them?
B) I don't see why not.
A) When can I try them?
B) As soon as I cook them up.
A) That sounds excellent.

Now practice the above conversation within your group. Use your own scenarios and say them out loud in English. Don't forget to involve all group members.

Listen to The Conversation T1

- What are you preparing?
- Some sweet and sour pork.
- You can make Chinese food?
- Sure. Why not? It's easy to make.

4) Happy Birthday T2

A)	**Happy Birthday, Michael.**
B)	**Thank you, Nancy.**
A)	**I baked you a birthday cake.**
B)	**It's a fabulous cake. Did your mother help you bake it?**
A)	**Not really. She simply gave me the recipe.**
B)	**Well, you did a marvelous job.**
A)	**Do you really think so?**
B)	**Oh, yes! It's really delicious.**

Now practice the above conversation within your group. Use your own scenarios and say them out loud in English. Don't forget to involve all group members.

5) Comprehension Activity

		True	False
1)	It's Nancy's birthday.	□	□
2)	Nancy baked the cake with her mother's help.	□	□
3)	Michael does not like the cake.	□	□
4)	Nancy does not want Michael to eat the cake.	□	□
5)	Nancy got the recipe from her father.	□	□
6)	The cake is for Nancy's mother.	□	□

6) The barbecued pork is wonderful.

Q	**This barbecued pork tastes wonderful.**
	Did you cook it up yourself?
A	**I sure did.**
Q	**What kind of barbecue sauce did you use?**
A	**I used Texas Ranch barbecue sauce.**
Q	**Where could I buy some?**
A	**At the supermarket.**

Now practice the above conversation within your group. Use your own scenarios and say them out loud in English. Don't forget to involve all group members.

7) Showing Agreement

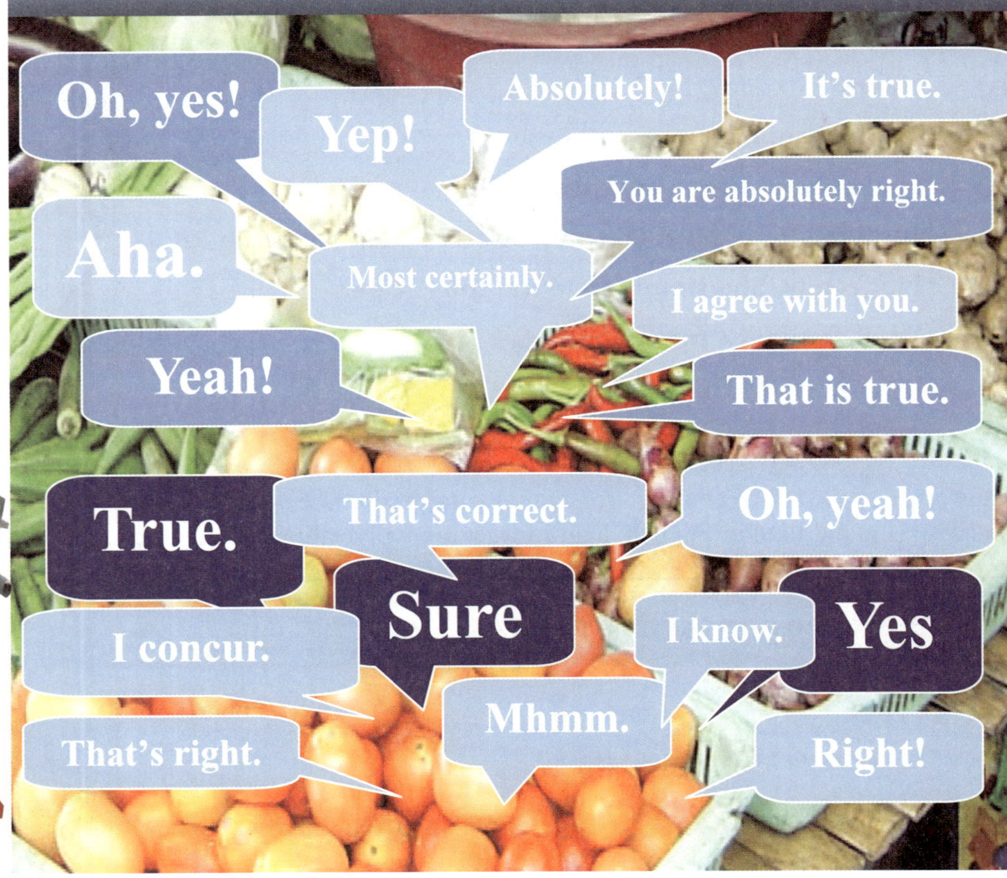

Now practice the above illustrated ways of agreeing. It is important that you know how to use and understand all of them. Don't forget to involve all group members.

8: a) What are you cooking? T3

to give a hand = to help

A) What are you cooking?

B) I'm cooking up some Hungarian goulash.

A) I know how to make goulash.

B) Good. You can give me a hand then.

A) Sorry, I don't have any time.

B) OK.

A) See you later then.

B) See you.

Now practice the above conversation within your group. Use your own scenarios and say them out loud in English. Don't forget to involve all group members.

8: b) Barbecue Cookout T4

A) I'd like to invite you to a barbecue cookout on Saturday afternoon.

B) I'd like that. What time should I be there?

A) We'll start at 4 pm.

B) What should I bring?

A) Can you bring some of those home made Hungarian sausages?

B) Sure. I'll see you at 4 then.

A) All right. See you then.

Use the conversation in activity 8 as a model for your conversations.

9) Home Made Cooking

A) I am cooking up some Mexican chilli. Are you interested in joining me for dinner?

B) When would you like me to join you?

A) Now.

B) I am sorry, but I am busy now.

A) How about tomorrow then?

B) Tomorrow sounds good.

Now take the given conversation and model your own conversations on it. Once again use your own scenarios.

"I am sorry, but I am busy now."

10) Pair Work (Will you have breakfast/lunch/dinner with me on ...?

Schedule 1

	Monday	Tuesday	Wednesday	Thursday	Friday	Saturday	Sunday
Morning	Busy	Busy	Free	Free	Busy	Busy	Busy
Afternoon	Free	Busy	Free	Busy	Busy	Free	Free
Evening	Busy	Free	Free	Busy	Busy	Busy	Free

One of you look at 'Schedule 1' on this page while the other turns to page 114 and looks at 'Schedule 2' in activity A). Take turns asking if certain times are good for the other student to have breakfast/lunch/dinner.

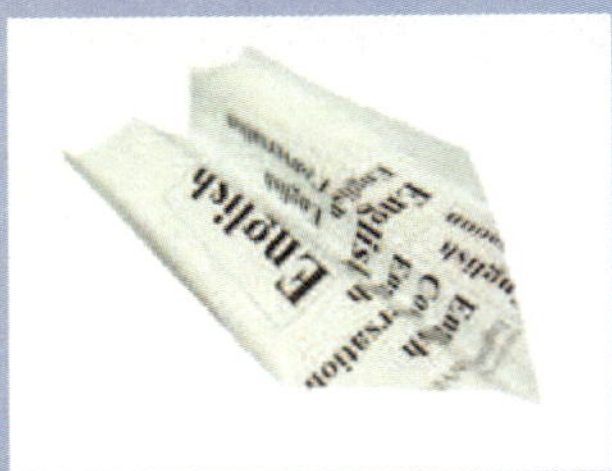

11: a) Fill in the missing information

Fill in the missing information by asking your group members for their answers to the following questions.

	Example	Friend 1	Friend 2
Name	Robert		
Are you free for lunch on Monday?	Yes, I am.		
Will you have dinner with me on Saturday afternoon?	I'm sorry, but I'm busy on Saturday.		
Will you join me for breakfast Friday morning?	Sure, I'd like that.		
Would you like to have dinner today?	No, I am busy.		

11: b) Listening Comprehension T5

Fill in the missing information by listening to the conversations.

	Betty	Tammy
Is she having breakfast, lunch or dinner with John?		
When is she having breakfast/ lunch/dinner with John?		
What is John cooking up for her?		

12: a) Write your own conversation (Would you like to have dinner with me?)

Write a conversation wherein you invite someone over to your home for dinner. Make sure to discuss times and the kinds of food you plan on cooking.

A) ______________________________

B) ______________________________

A) ______________________________

B) ______________________________

A) ______________________________

B) ______________________________

A) ______________________________

B) ______________________________

Now act out the conversations you wrote with your group members. Remember to involve all group members.

12: b) Write your own conversation (What are you cooking?)

Write a conversation wherein you ask someone about what they are cooking or baking.

A) ______________________________

B) ______________________________

A) ______________________________

B) ______________________________

A) ______________________________

B) ______________________________

A) ______________________________

B) ______________________________

"What are you barbecuing?"

12: c) I baked this cake for you.

Write a conversation about baking a cake for someone's birthday.

____

____

____

____

____

____

____

13) Puzzle

Use the sentences found in Unit 4 to help you complete the following puzzle.

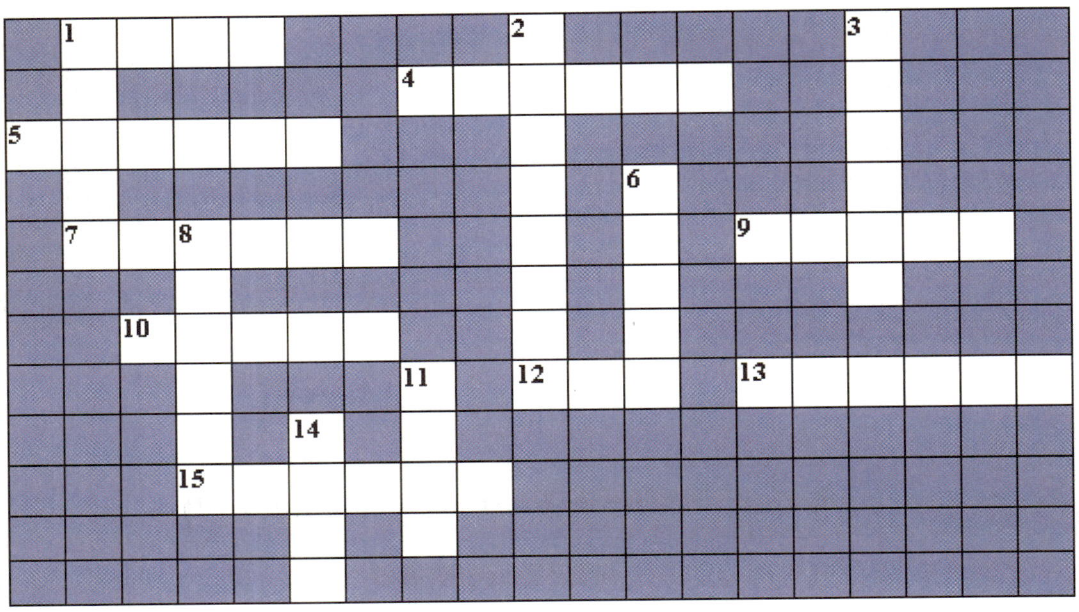

After you have completed the puzzle, check the 'Puzzle Solutions' section at the back of the book for the solution to the above puzzle.

Across

1) As ________ as I cook them up.
4) Do you ____________ think so?
5) What are you ____________?
7) The pork ____________ wonderful?
9) See you _________ then.
10) I am ________ but I am busy now.
12) I don't ________ why not.
13) Tomorrow _________ good.
15) Will you have __________ with me on Saturday?

Down

1) I'll _______ up the barbecue.
2) It's a ____________ cake.
3) I'd like to _________ you to a barbecue.
6) ________ can I buy some?
8) What time ________ I be there?
11) Are you ________ for lunch?
14) I _________ how to make goulash.

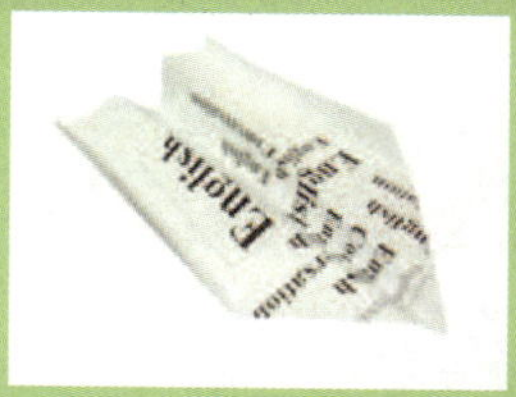

BUSINESS NAME

Unit 5

Cash for a Living

Grammar

Content

- Dual Meaning Words ('Bills' and 'Bills')
- Various Uses of 'So'

Unit breakdown:

Breaking Bills and Shopping	**p. 40**
Paying Bills & Withdrawing	**p. 41**
Banking Terminologies	**p. 42**
Using an ATM	**p. 43**
Comprehension Activities	**p. 44**
Review Activities	**p. 45**
Puzzle	**p. 46**

Banking and Internet Banking

This unit focuses on …

- Banking terminologies
- Making withdrawals
- Using an ATM
- Transferring money
- Using debit cards

Break Bill

1) Can you break some bills?

A) Can you break some bills?

B) How much would you like to break?

A) 10,000 won.

B) Sorry. I don't have any small bills. You should try the variety store to see if they can break that bill for you.

A) Yes, that's not a bad idea at all.

B) Sure. Why don't you try your luck?

good idea = not a bad idea

Now practice the above conversation within your group. Use your own scenarios and say them out loud in English. Don't forget to involve all group members.

"Let's go shopping for some school supplies."

2) Could I borrow some money?

A) How much money do you have?

B) Why do you ask?

A) I'd like to go to the mall with you.

B) What for?

A) I'd like to buy a new pair of jeans.

B) Don't you have enough money?

A) No. Could I borrow some money from you?

B) How much do you need?

A) It costs about a hundred dollars for a new pair of jeans.

B) Really. That's too much. I don't have so much.

A) That's too bad.

B) I can lend you twenty dollars. Is that enough?

A) Well, I guess it is. Thanks.

Now practice the above conversation within your group. Use your own scenarios and say them out loud in English. Don't forget to involve all group members.

---

3) Listen to The Conversation T1

- Do you feel like going shopping to the mall?
- Sure. What would you like to buy?
- Some new clothes for the new semester.
- Sounds good. Let's go then.

4) Withdrawing and Transferring T2

A) **Mindy. Let's go to the bank.**

B) **Why do you want to go Sue? Do you need some money?**

A) **Yes, I'd like to withdraw 100 dollars, but I only have 50 dollars in my account.**

B) **Really? I could transfer 50 dollars into your account so you could have enough.**

A) **Would you do that for me?**

B) **Sure.**

A) **All right then. Let's go.**

B) **OK.**

Now practice the above conversation within your group. Use your own scenarios and say them out loud in English. Don't forget to involve all group members.

5) Listening Comprehension

		True	False
1)	Mindy needs money.	□	□
2)	Sue asks Mindy for money.	□	□
3)	Sue wants to withdraw 50 dollars.	□	□
4)	Mindy offers to give Sue 50 dollars.	□	□
5)	Mindy offers to transfer 100 dollars into Sue's account.	□	□
6)	Sue wants to deposit 50 dollars into Mindy's account.	□	□
7)	Mindy goes to the bank with Sue.	□	□

"Would you like to go to the bank?"

"Sure. Let's go."

6) Paying Bills

Q **I need to pay my utility bills.**

A **Do you have enough money?**

Q **Yes. Of course.**

A **How do you pay your bills?**

Q **I need to deposit money into a designated account.**

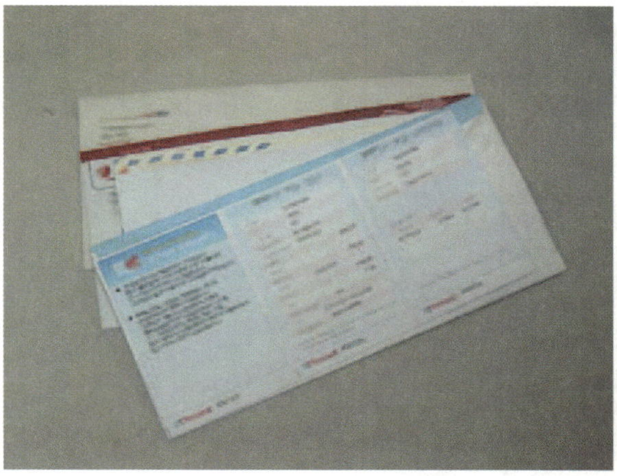

Now practice the above conversation within your group. Use your own scenarios and say them out loud in English. Don't forget to involve all group members.

7) Banking Terms

Pin numbers are the secret numbers used to access one's bank account

Now practice the above banking vocabulary. It is important that you know how to use and understand all of them. Don't forget to involve all group members.

8: a) Internet Banking T3

A) Can you transfer some money into my account?

B) It's too late. The banks are closed.

A) Why don't you use internet banking then?

B) That's a good idea. How much should I transfer?

A) I need $200.

B) That's too much. What do you need the money for?

A) I have to buy some books for school.

B) Are books so expensive?

A) Yes, they are.

B) Oh my! All right. I'll do it tonight then.

Now practice the above conversation within your group. Use your own scenarios and say them out loud in English. Don't forget to involve all group members.

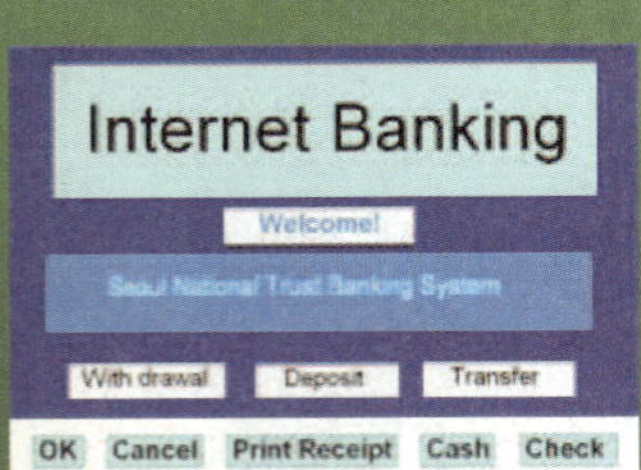

8: b) Using an ATM T4

A) I am going out to use the bank machine.

B) What is a bank machine?

A) It's an ATM.

B) An ATM?

A) Yes! An Automated Teller Machine.

B) What does this machine do?

A) You can use it to take money out of your bank account.

B) Really? That sounds good.

A) All you need is a bank card and your secret pin number.

B) Is that all?

Now use the conversation in activity 8 as a model for your conversations.

9) Banks and Account Numbers

A) What is your account number?

B) It's 1-2-3-7-6-5-9-0-8-4-3-2-7-6-5-4.

A) And your name please?

B) My name is Mark Johnson.

A) Could I have the name of your Bank?

B) Seoul National Trust Bank.

A) Good. That's everything. Thank you.

"What is your account number?"

Now take the given conversation and model your own conversations on it. Once again use your own information.

10) Fill in the missing information

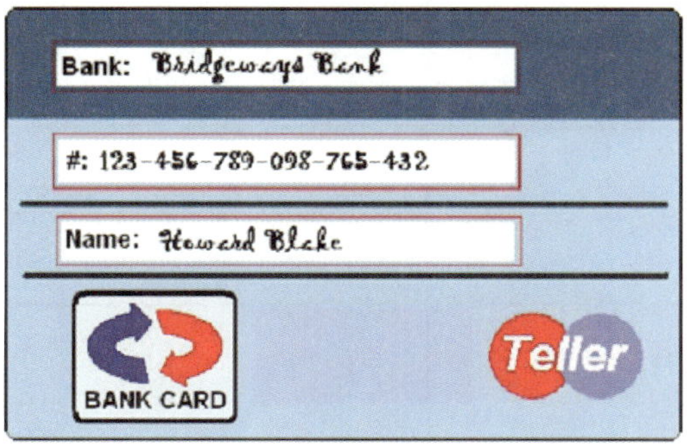

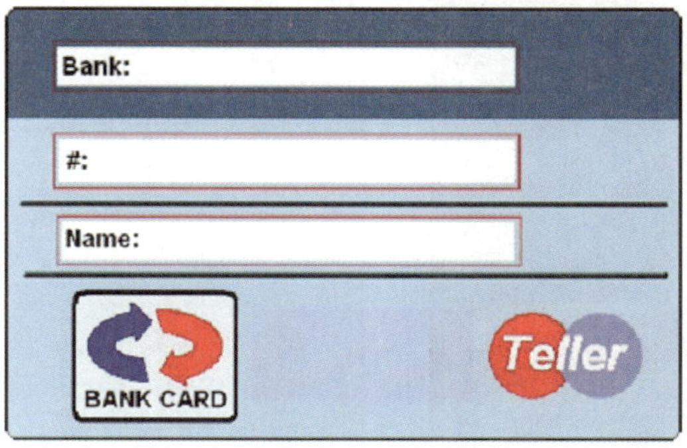

Now take turns filling in the missing information on the second card. Create a bank name and a bank account number. Don't use your real information.

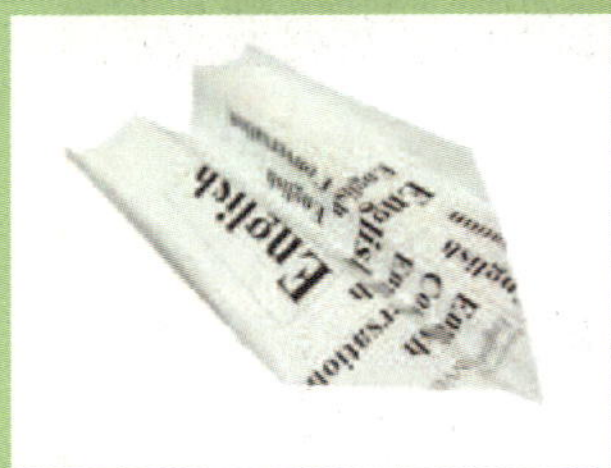

11: a) Fill in the missing information

Fill in the missing information by asking your group members some questions.

	Example	Friend 1	Friend 2	Friend 3
Name	Ben Taylor			
Account Number	234-987-456-123			
Deposit Amount	500 dollars			
Transfer Amount	150 dollars			
Account Number for Transfer	357-975-135-753			

A) What is your account number?
B) My account number is 234-987-456-123.

A) How much will you be depositing today?
B) I'd like to deposit 500 dollars.

A) Would you like to perform any additional transactions?
B) Yes. I'd like to transfer 150 dollars.

A) What's the number of the account you would like to transfer the money to?
B) 357-975-135-753

11: b) Listening Comprehension T5

Fill in the missing information by listening to the conversations.

	Serena	Gabriella
How much does she want to deposit?		
How much does she want to transfer?		
What is the number of the account she wants to transfer to?		

12: a) Write your own conversation (Depositing Money)

Write about depositing money into someone's bank account.

A) ______________________________

B) ______________________________

A) ______________________________

B) ______________________________

A) ______________________________

B) ______________________________

A) ______________________________

B) ______________________________

A) ______________________________

Now act out the conversations you wrote with your group members. Remember to involve all group members.

12: b) Write your own conversation (Transferring Money)

Write a conversation about using internet banking for transferring money, then act it out with your group.

A) ______________________________

B) ______________________________

A) ______________________________

B) ______________________________

A) ______________________________

B) ______________________________

A) ______________________________

B) ______________________________

"How much would you like to transfer?"

12: c) Withdrawing with an ATM

Write about withdrawing money using an ATM.

____

____

____

____

____

____

____

13) Puzzle

Use the sentences found in Unit 5 to help you complete the following puzzle.

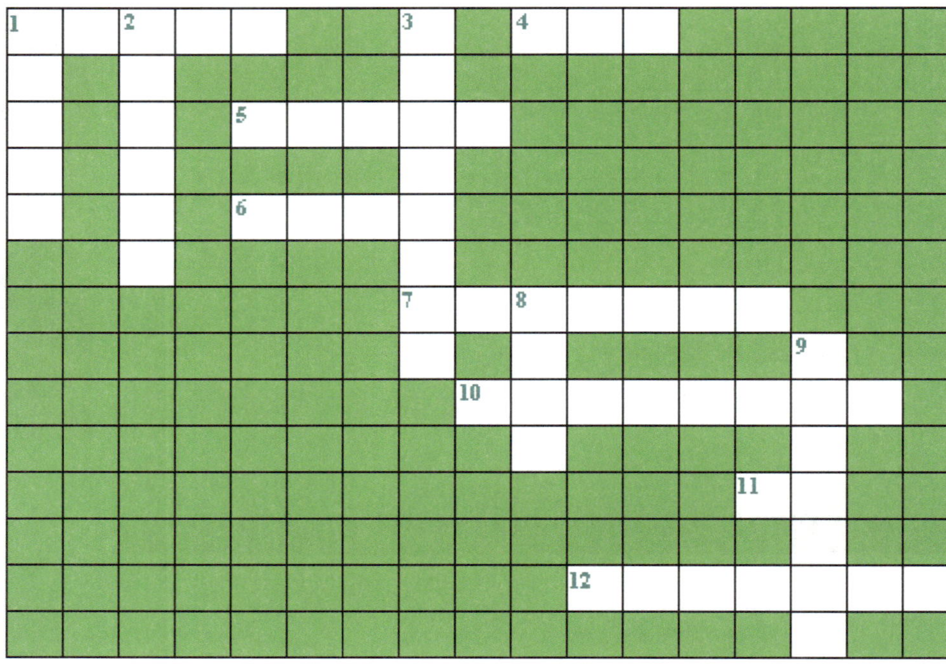

After you have completed the puzzle, check the 'Puzzle Solutions' section at the back of the book for the solution to the above puzzle.

Across

1) Can you _______ some large bills?
4) What is your secret _____ number?
5) It _______ 100 dollars.
6) Do you ________ some money?
7) Bank __________
10) Can you _____________ 50 dollars into my account?
11) Are books ___ expensive?
12) Why don't you use internet __________?

Down

1) I don't have any small _______.
2) Don't you have ________ money?
3) I'd like to __________ 50 dollars.
8) Debit _______
9) I'd like to __________ my whole paycheck into my account.

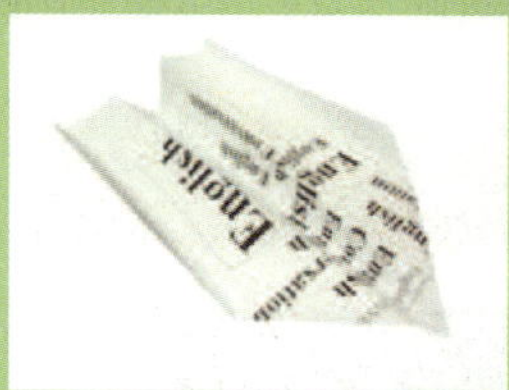

BUSINESS NAME

Unit 6
Public Transportation

Getting Around

Grammar Content

- Comparative Adjectives
- Superlative Adjectives
- Auxiliaries
- The Conjunction 'While'

Unit breakdown:

Comparative Adjectives p. 48
Comprehension Activities p. 49
Taking the Train p. 50
Transportation Terms p. 51
Listening Activities p. 52
Review Activities p. 53
Puzzle p. 54

Public Transit

This unit focuses on ...

- The different modes of transportation
- Getting around using public transportation
- Transportation terminologies
- Asking people how to get to places

High Speed Train

1) Which bus goes to the park?

A) Excuse me. Could you tell me which bus goes to Central Park?
B) Yes. Take bus number 001.

A) How long is the trip?
B) It's about 15 minutes.

A) Thank you for the info.
B) Not a problem.

info = information

Now practice the above conversation within your group. Use your own scenarios and say them out loud in English. Don't forget to include all your group members.

2) Id like to get there as fast as possible.

"I'd like to get there as fast as I can."

A) Should we go to Pusan City?
B) When would you like to go?
A) How about next week?
B) I don't see why not.
A) Why don't we go for 2 days?
B) OK.
A) Let's take the bus.
B) No. Taking the high speed train is better.
A) Really?
B) Yes. I'd like to get there as soon as possible.
A) Is the high speed train much faster?
B) Yes. The trip by bus takes 4 hours while the high speed train takes only 2 hours.
A) Oh good.

Now practice the above conversation within your group. Use your own scenarios and say them out loud in English. Don't forget to involve all group members.

3) Listen to The Conversation T1

- The high speed train is really fast.
- Is it faster than the bus?
- Oh yes. It's much faster than the bus.
- Oh! I didn't know the bus was so much slower.

4) You should take the train. T2

A) **Jack. How do you get to Branford from here?**

B) **You should take the train, Jess.**

A) **Where is the train station?**

B) **Just take bus number 5 and go 3 stops till you get to Main Station.**

A) **OK. Where is the bus stop?**

B) **Go straight two blocks, then turn left. It should be on your right hand side.**

A) **That sounds easy enough. Thank you, Jack.**

B) **You're welcome, Jess.**

Now practice the above conversation within your group. Use your own scenarios and say them out loud in English. Don't forget to involve all group members.

5) Comprehension Activity

	True	False
1) Jess wants to go to Branford.	☐	☐
2) Jack tells Jess to go to Branford by bus.	☐	☐
3) Jack tells Jess to go to Branford by train.	☐	☐
4) Jess needs to take bus number 3 and go 5 stops.	☐	☐
5) Jess thinks getting to the bus station is easy.	☐	☐
6) Jack thinks Jess should not go to Branford.	☐	☐

"How do I get to Branford?"

"You can take the train."

6) Taking the Ferry

Q **I'd like to take my car to Cheju Island.**

A **Why don't you take the ferry then?**

Q **Does the ferry take cars?**

A **It sure does.**

Q **Well, I should go by ferry then.**

A **Yes, you should.**

Now practice the above conversation within your group. Use your own scenarios and say them out loud in English. Don't forget to involve all group members.

7) Transportation Terminology

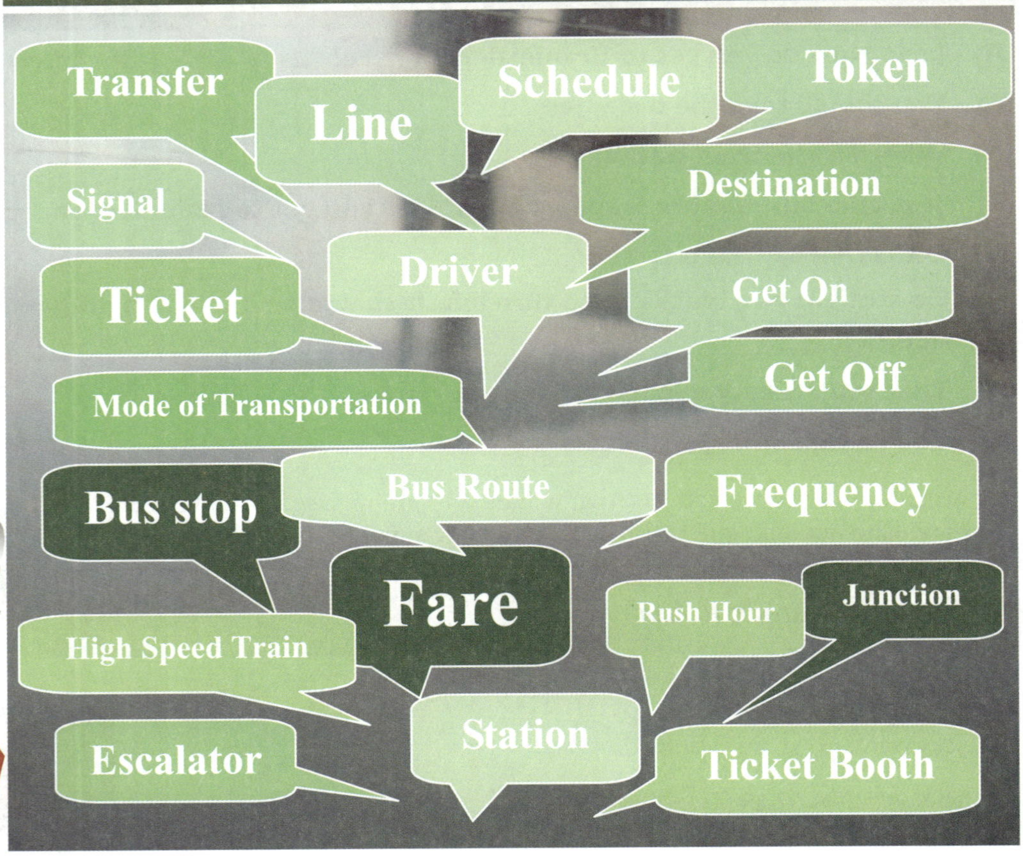

Now practice the above illustrated travel terminology. It is important that you know how to use and understand all of them. Don't forget to involve all group members.

8: a) Taking The Subway T3

A) I'd like to get to Main Market. Can you tell me how to get there by subway?

B) You need to take line number 5 and go 6 stops to Lawrence Station, then transfer to line number 4. Main Market is two stops from there.

A) Do you know how much the fare is these days?

B) One token is 2 dollars.

A) A token?

B) Yes. Instead of tickets, you need tokens to ride on the subway.

A) Is that so?

B) Yes it is.

Now practice the above conversation within your group. Use your own scenarios and say them out loud in English. Don't forget to involve all group members.

8: b) What's the fastest way to city hall? T4

A) What's the fastest way to get to City Hall?

B) It's rush hour now, so driving is too slow. You should take the subway.

A) How do I get to Market Square Station from First Station?

B) Go four stops to Baseline Junction, then transfer to line number 2 and go one more station.

A) Oh, that's easy. Thank you.

B) You're welcome.

Check the 'Supplementary Materials' section at the back of the book (p.115) for a larger map.

Now ask your group members how to get to places on the map.

9) Getting Around by Subway

A) Excuse me! How do I get to College Station from Triangle Junction?

B) Go two stops to Sports Complex Junction, then transfer to line 2 and go two more stops to College Station.

A) That's easy. Thanks.

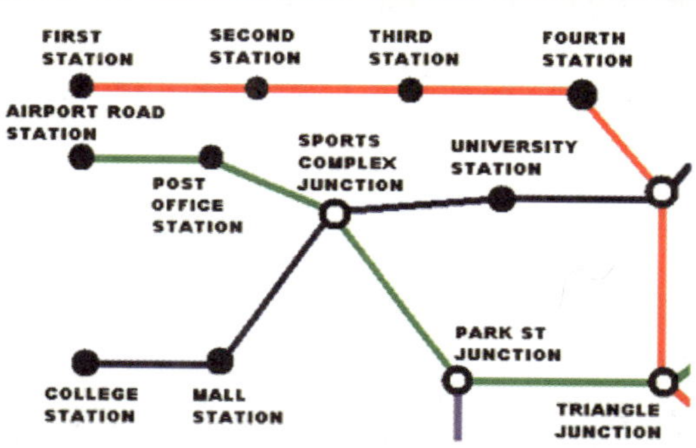

"Excuse me! How can I get to College Station?"

Now take the given conversation and model your own conversations on it. Use the map on page 115.

10) Fill in the missing information

Example	Friend
How do I get to City Hall from First Station?	**How do I get to ____________ from ____________?**
Take line number 1 to Baseline Junction, then transfer to line number 2 and go 4 stops to City Hall.	

Now take turns filling in the missing information. Use the map on page 115.

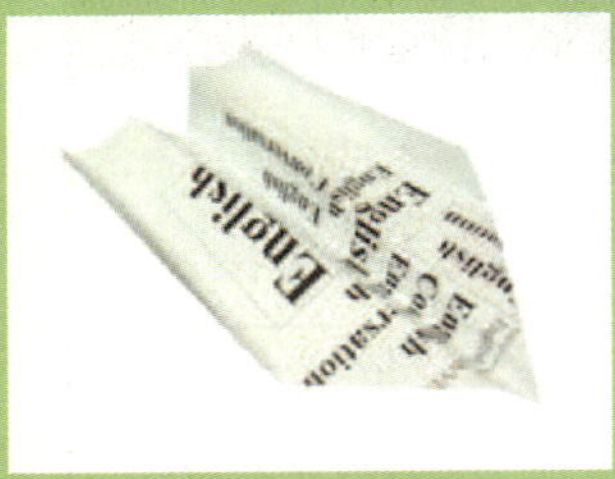

11: a) Fill in the missing information

Fill in the missing information by asking your friends some questions.

	Destination	Directions
Example	First Station → Park junction	Get on line number 1 and go 5 stations till you get to Triangle Junction, then transfer to line number 3 and go 1 stop to Park Street Junction.
Friend 1	Zoo Station → Eighth Station	
Friend 2	Fire Station → Tenth Station	
Friend 3	Union Station → Museum Station	

A) Excuse me. Can you tell me how to get to Park Junction from First Station?

B) Get on line number 1 and go 5 stations till you get to Triangle Junction ,then transfer to line number 3 and go1 stop to Park Street Junction.

11: b) Listening Comprehension T5

Fill in the missing information by listening to the conversations.

	Angelina	Kate
What is her mode of transportation ?		
What is her transfer point?		
How many stops does she need to go?		

12: a) Write your own conversation (Could you tell me ..?)

Write a conversation wherein you ask someone how to take the subway or bus to any local destination. Use the subway map on page 115.

A) ______________________________
B) ______________________________
A) ______________________________
B) ______________________________
A) ______________________________
B) ______________________________
A) ______________________________
B) ______________________________

Now act out the conversations you wrote with your group members.

12: b) Write your own conversation (By Air or By Ferry)

Write a conversation wherein you ask someone how to get to any destination by air or by ferry.

A) ______________________________
B) ______________________________
A) ______________________________
B) ______________________________
A) ______________________________
B) ______________________________
A) ______________________________
B) ______________________________

"Excuse me. Could you tell me how to get to Cheju Island by ferry?"

12: c) Getting to School

Write about how you get to school every day.

____
____
____
____
____
____
____

13) Puzzle

Use the sentences found in Unit 6 to help you complete the following puzzle.

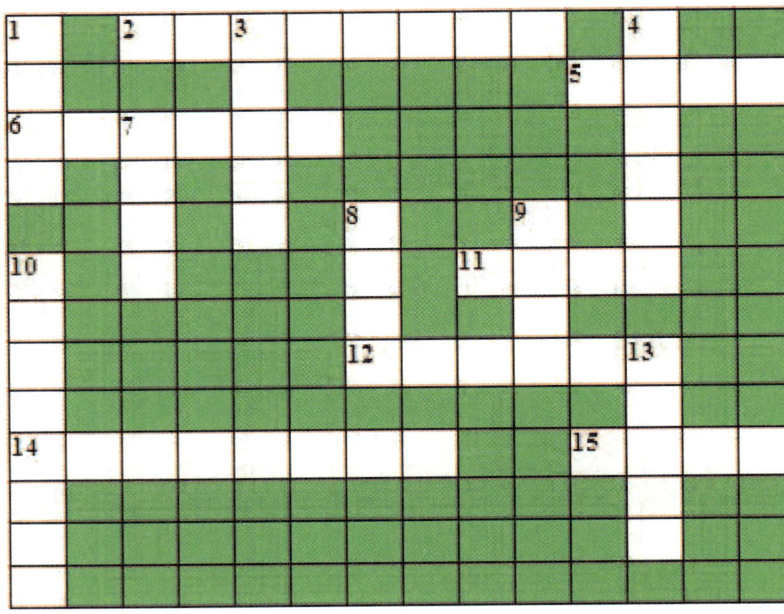

After you have completed the puzzle, check the 'Puzzle Solutions' section at the back of the book for the solution to the above puzzle.

Across

2) As soon as ____________.

5) The train is faster ________ the bus.

6) Take bus __________ 6.

11) It will be on your right _________ side.

12) Instead of tickets, you need ________ to ride the subway.

14) Go ___________ two blocks.

15) It's rush ________, so traffic is pretty bad.

Down

1) How _______ is the trip?

3) High _________ Train

4) You __________ take the bus.

7) The train is _________ faster.

8) Is _______ so?

9) How much is the _______ these days?

10) You have to ___________ at Triangle Junction.

13) It's only 4 ________ to First Station.

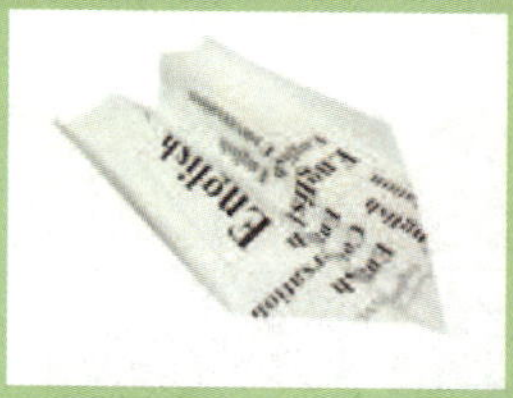

Unit 7

Computers in Daily Life

Grammar Content

- The Various uses of 'So'
- The conjunction 'But'
- The Preposition 'For'

Unit breakdown:

Printing Documents	**p. 56**
Clicking and Saving	**p. 57**
Computer Terminology	**p. 58**
Adjusting the Monitor	**p. 59**
Comprehensi on Activities	**p. 60**
Review Activities	**p. 61**
Puzzle	**p. 62**

I'm Addicted to Computers

This unit focuses on ...

- Computer terminology
- Providing and asking for assistance in using a computer
- Using a computer and other peripheral devices
- The type of activities and jobs computers are used for
- Asking questions about the frequency of events

Print Sheet

1) Print this out for me.

A) Will you print this document for me?
B) OK. Do you want it in color?

A) No. Black and white will do.
B) Are you sure?

A) Yes. I just need it for my records.
B) It'll take a few minutes.

A) That's all right.
B) I'll have it for you really soon.

will do = is fine

Now practice the above conversation within your group. Use your own scenarios and say them out loud in English. Don't forget to involve all group members.

"Oh my! The printer is down."

2) The printer is down.

A) Oh my! The printer is down and I can't print a thing.
B) Did you turn the printer on?
A) I don't know. Where do I turn it on?
B) The power switch is at the back of the printer.
A) I can't find it. Can you help me?
B) Sure. There you go.
A) Thank you.
B) Is it working now?
A) Let me try it again.
B) There you are. It seems to be working fine.
A) Yes. It works fine now. Thank you so much dear.
B) Any time mom.

Now practice the above conversation within your group. Use your own scenarios and say them out loud in English. Don't forget to involve all group members.

3) Listen to the conversation T1

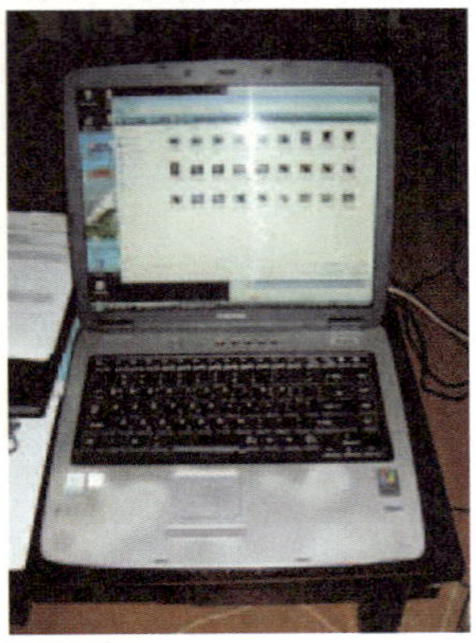

- **This notebook is so small.**
- **Yes. But it can do everything the desktop can do.**
- **Is that so?**
- **Yes. That is correct.**

4) Just click on the mouse T2

A) **Jessie, I'd like to enter my name. How do I do it?**

B) **Just click on the entry box with your mouse and start typing.**

A) **I'm clicking but nothing's happening.**

B) **You need to click the left button. You're clicking the wrong one. Try your other left.**

A) **I see. Good then. Now, how do I get to the next line?**

B) **Just press the ENTER key.**

A) **Like this?**

B) **Yes. Just like that Peter.**

Now practice the above conversation within your group. Use your own scenarios and say them out loud in English. Don't forget to involve all group members.

5) Comprehension activity

		True	False
1)	Peter does not know how to enter his name.	□	□
2)	Jessie tells Peter to press the right mouse button.	□	□
3)	Peter learns to press the left mouse button.	□	□
4)	Jessie tells Peter to press space bar to get to the next line.	□	□
5)	Peter can't get to the next line, even with Peter's help.	□	□
6)	Jessie tells Peter to click the right ENTER button.	□	□

6) Saving to your hard drive

Q **Don't forget to save your files.**

A **But my hard drive is full.**

Q **Use this external hard drive.**

A **Does it work the same?**

Q **Yes. But first you have to plug it in.**

A **All right.**

Now practice the above conversation within your group. Use your own scenarios and say them out loud in English. Don't forget to involve all group members.

7) Computer terminology

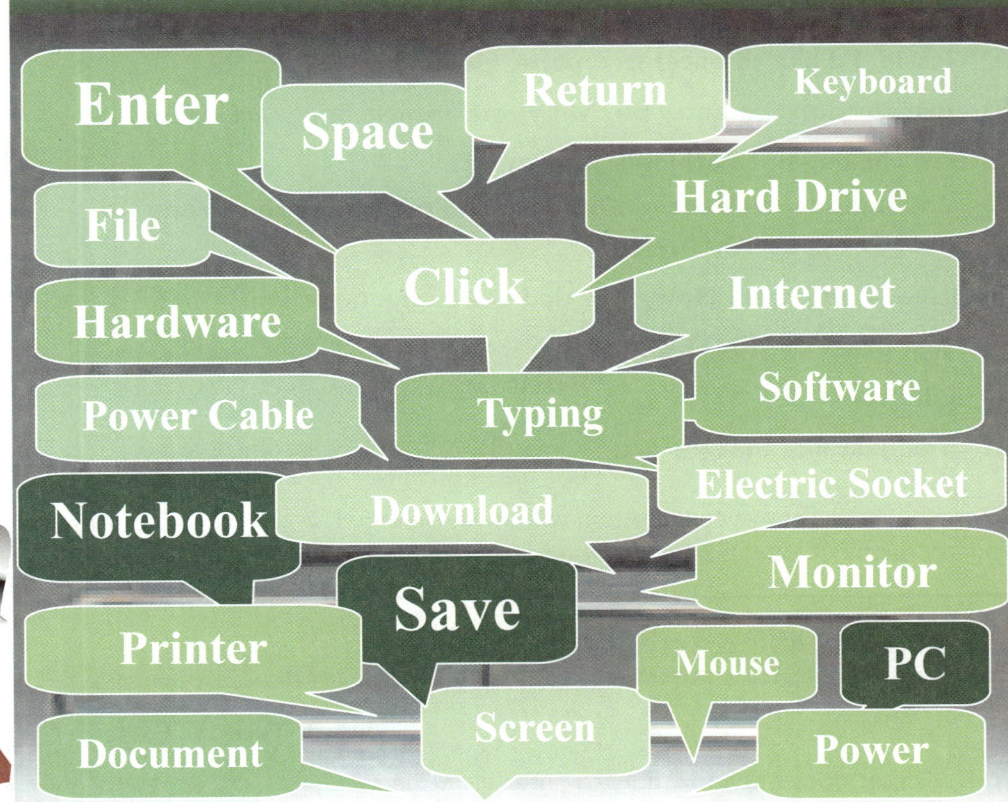

PC = Personal Computer (Desk Top Computer)

Now practice the above illustrated computer terminology. It's important that you know how to use and understand all of them. Don't forget to involve all group members.

8: a) Press the ENTER key. T3

A) Press the ENTER key.

B) Where is that?

A) It's on the keyboard.

B) Yes, I know. But where exactly is it?

A) It's right there under your right pinky.

B) Oh! There it is.

A) You should be more attentive.

B) Give me a break.

Now practice the above conversation within your group. Use your own scenarios and say them out loud in English. Don't forget to involve all group members.

8: b) Can you plug in this monitor? T4

A) Can you please plug in this monitor?

B) Sorry. I am busy. But you can do it yourself by plugging one end of that power cable into the back of the monitor and the other end into the electric socket.

A) OK. ... There we go.

B) I knew you could do it.

A) Yes. But how do I turn it on?

B) Simply press the power button.

A) Where is that?

B) It's the large button on the front of the monitor.

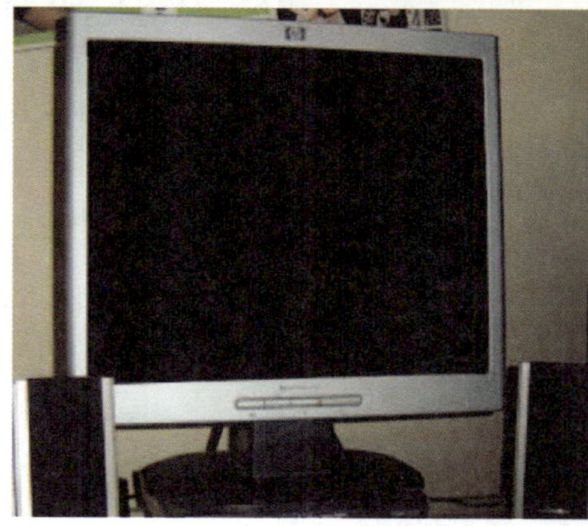

Use the conversation in activity 8 as a model for your conversations.

9) My monitor is too bright.

A) Stacey, my monitor is too bright.

B) You should adjust it then.

A) OK. Easier said than done.

B) Press the menu button, and adjust the brightness.

A) I see. ... There we go.

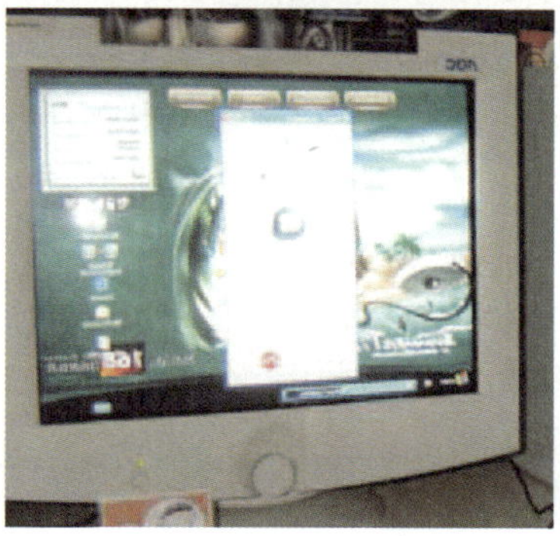

"Easier said than done."
(That's not so easy.)

Now take the given conversation and model your own conversations on it.

10) Fill in the missing information

If the speakers are too loud, you need to adjust the;

□ Sharpness □ Volume □ Brightness

If the monitor is too bright, you need to adjust the;

□ Sharpness □ Volume □ Brightness

If the printer is not on, you need to press;

□ ENTER □ Power □ Shift

If you want to get to the next line in a document, you need to press;

□ ENTER □ Power □ Shift

Put a check next to the correct response.

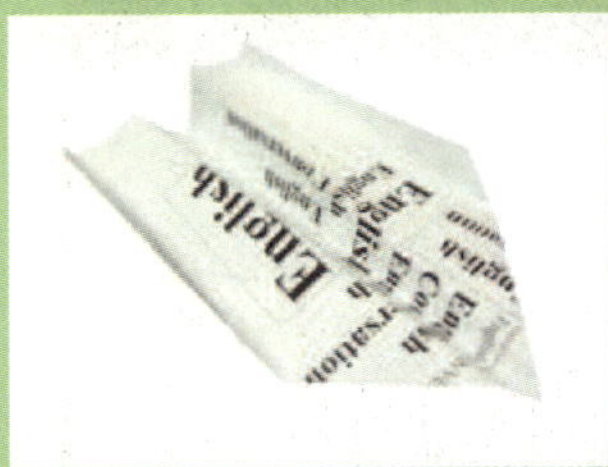

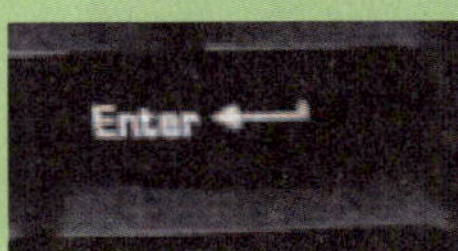

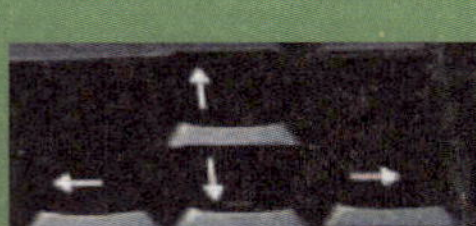

11: a) Fill in the missing information

Fill in the missing information by asking your friends some questions.

	Example	Friend 1	Friend 2	Friend 3
Name	Brian			
Do you prefer PCs or notebooks?	I prefer notebooks.			
What do you use your computer for?	To surf the internet.			
How often do you use a computer?	Every day.			
Do you watch movies on your computer?	Yes, of course.			

11: b) Listening Comprehension T5

Fill in the missing information by listening to the conversations.

	Maggie	Sally
What does she usually use computers for?		
How often does she use a computer?		
Does she own a notebook or a PC?		

12: a) Write your own conversation (How do you check your e-mail?)

Write about asking someone how to use a specific function on a computer.

A) ______________________________
B) ______________________________
A) ______________________________
B) ______________________________
A) ______________________________
B) ______________________________
A) ______________________________
B) ______________________________

Now act out the conversations you wrote with your group members. Remember to involve all group members.

12: b) Write your own conversation (What do you use computers for?)

Write a conversation wherein you ask someone what s/he uses her/his computer for, and ask her/him how often s/he uses it.

A) ______________________________
B) ______________________________
A) ______________________________
B) ______________________________
A) ______________________________
B) ______________________________
A) ______________________________
B) ______________________________

"How often do you usually use computers?"

12: c) How do you turn on a computer?

Write a conversation wherein you teach someone how to use a computer.

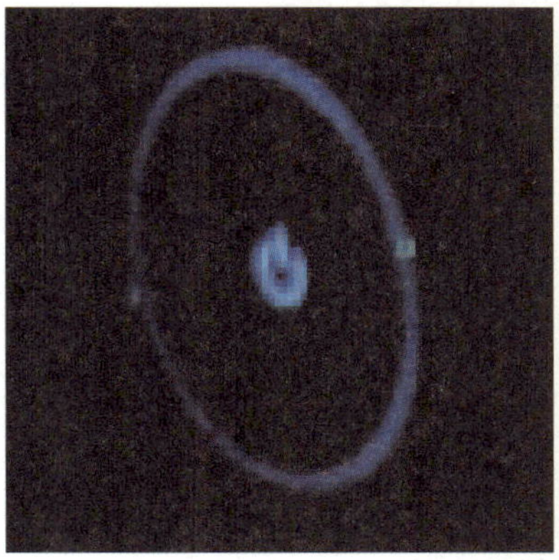

____
____
____
____
____
____
____

13) Puzzle

Use the sentences found in Unit 7 to help you complete the following puzzle.

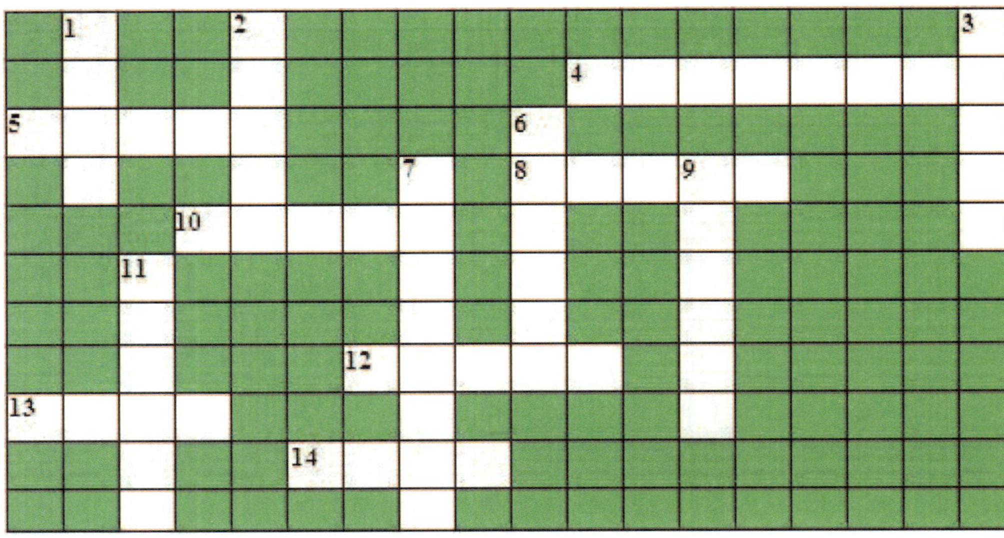

After you have completed the puzzle, check the 'Puzzle Solutions' section at the back of the book for the solution to the above puzzle.

Across

4) ____________ Computer
5) Will you __________ this document for me?
8) How _________ do you use your computer?
10) Hard __________
12) Push the __________ button to turn on the computer.
13) First you need to _________ it in.
14) I use the computer to _________ the internet.

Down

1) Did you ______ on the monitor?
2) I'd like to ________ my name.
3) You need to ________ on the mouse.
6) Would you please turn down the _________?
7) The _____________ is used to enter data.
9) It's _________ said than done.
11) How do I ___________ the brightness?

Unit 8

Music Is My Life

BUSINESS NAME

Grammar

Content

- Casual Language in Real Contexts
- Slang Expressions

Unit breakdown:

Playing Music & Instruments p. 64

Live Music & Concerts p. 65

Music Terminology p. 66

Music Genres & Selections p. 67

Comprehension Activities p. 68

Review Activities p. 69

Puzzle p. 70

Let's Listen to Some Music

This unit focuses on ...

- Music terminology
- Music genres
- Musical instruments
- Conversation about concert venues
- Selecting the right music

Electric Guitar

1) Guitars are my life.

A) Can you play the guitar?
B) Yes. I'm crazy about guitars.

A) So, you must be able to play well.
B) Yes. I am in a Rock & Roll band.

A) Wow! Do you perform live?
B) Yes. We are playing this Saturday.

A) Will you invite me?
B) Of course.

I'm crazy about guitars = I love guitars very much

Now practice the above conversation within your group. Use your own scenarios and say them out loud in English. Don't forget to include all your group members.

---

2) Playing The Guitar

"Every single day."

A) How often do you play the guitar?
B) Every single day.
A) Can you play now?
B) I don't have my guitar here.
A) Here! Why don't you use mine?
B) OK.
A) Here it is.
B) This is an acoustic guitar.
A) Is that a problem?
B) No. But I usually play electric guitars.
A) Can you play on the acoustic guitar?
B) All right. I'll give it a go.
A) Let's hear you play then.
B) ♪♫♫♪...
A) That is awesome.
B) You think so?
A) Yeah!

Now practice the above conversation within your group. Use your own scenarios and say them out loud in English. Don't forget to include all group members.

---

3) Listen to The Conversation T1

- **I can only play this bongo.**
- **Let's hear you play it then.**
- **OK. I'll give it a go. ♪♫♪♪♫♪...**
- **That's not too bad. Can I give it a go?**

4) Live Music Rocks T2

It rocks = It's awesome

A) Hey, Benny!

B) Yeah Jimmy, what's up?

A) This band really rocks.

B) It sure does. It's an awesome band. They're from Seoul.

A) Hey Benny! Do you want to start a band with me?

B) I don't know. I can't play any musical instruments.

A) Well, you can sing, can't you?

B) A little, but not well enough to be in a band.

Now practice the above conversation within your group. Use your own scenarios and say them out loud in English. Don't forget to involve all group members.

"You can sing, can't you?"

"Yeah. But not well."

5) Comprehension Activity

		True	False
1)	Jimmy thinks the band really rocks.	□	□
2)	Jimmy does not like the band at all.	□	□
3)	Benny wants to start a band.	□	□
4)	Jimmy does not want to start a band.	□	□
5)	Benny can't play any musical instruments.	□	□
6)	Benny can sing really well.	□	□

6) Reggae music is not my favorite.

Q This Reggae band really rocks.

A I don't know about that.

Q Don't you like reggae music?

A No. Reggae music is not my favorite.

Q What kind of music do you like then?

A I like rock music.

Now practice the above conversation within your group. Use your own scenarios and say them out loud in English. Don't forget to involve all group members.

7) Music Genres and Music Terminology

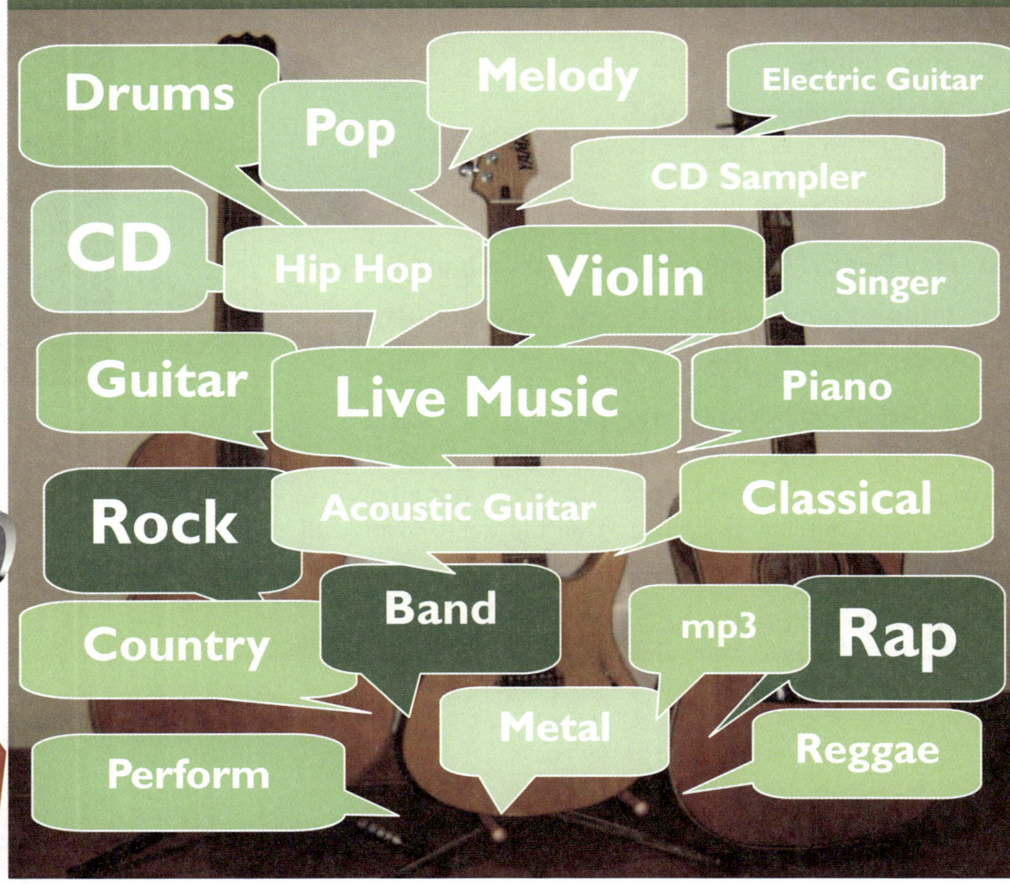

Now practice the above illustrated music terms. It is important that you know how to use and understand all of them. Don't forget to involve all group members.

8: a) I Love Classic Rock T3

A) Put on some classic rock music.

B) Have you ever heard of ZPJ?

A) Sure. ZPJ is amazing.

B) I'll put on some ZPJ then.

A) Why don't you put on the song 'A Love That's So Unfair"?

B) That's a really nice one.

A) Yes. Now turn up the volume.

B) OK.

Now practice the above conversation within your group. Use your own scenarios and say them out loud in English. Don't forget to involve all group members.

8: b) There is a large selection of music. T4

A) There is a large selection of music here. I can't seem to select a CD.

B) Well, what kind of music do you like?

A) All kinds really.

B) Do you have a favorite band then?

A) I really like The Beatles.

B) But they're so old.

A) Yes, but their music is still very nice.

B) I think I have to agree with you on that one.

Use the conversation in activity 8 as a model for your conversations.

9) The CD Sampler

A) I'd like to listen to this CD but I don't want to buy it.

B) You should listen to it on the CD sampler then.

A) How do I do that?

B) Just click on the song name you want to listen to and it will play the song for you.

A) Nice. I'll do just that then.

Now take the given conversation and model your own conversations on it. Once again use your own scenarios.

"I'd like to listen to this CD without actually buying it."

10) Fill in the missing information

Example	Friend
Do you play any musical instruments?	**Do you play any musical instruments?**
I play the guitar.	
How often do you watch movies?	**How often do you watch movies?**
I watch a movie a week.	

Now take turns filling in the missing information by asking your friends some questions.

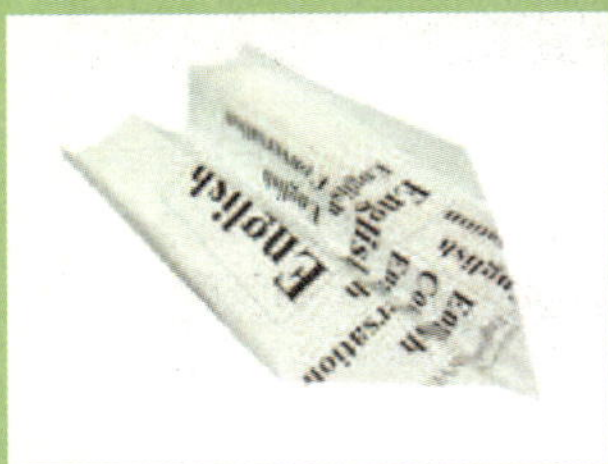

11: a) Fill in the missing information

Fill in the missing information by asking your friends some questions.

	Example	Friend 1	Friend 2	Friend 3
Name	Arnold			
Do you play a musical instrument?	Yes. I play the violin.			
What is your favourite genre of music?	I love Hip Hop.			
Do you like to listen to live music?	Yes. Live music rocks.			
How often do you listen to live music?	Every Single Weekend.			

11: b) Listening Comprehension T5

Fill in the missing information by listening to the conversations.

	Daniel	Larry
Does he play a musical instrument?		
Does he play in a band?		
What kind of music does he play?		

12: a) Write your own conversation (Do you listen to ..?)

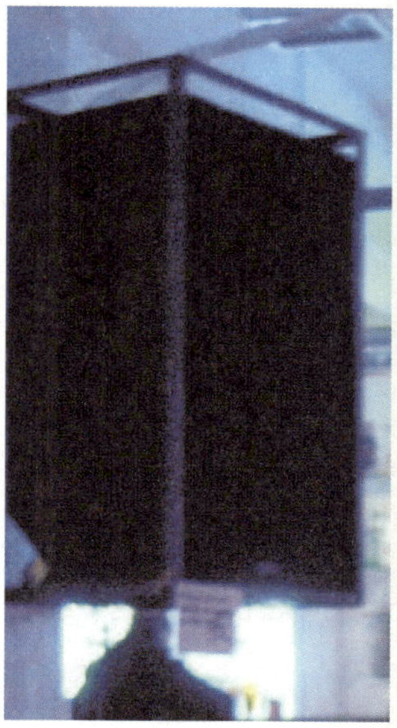

Write a conversation wherein you ask someone what kind of music s/he listens to.

A) ______________________________

B) ______________________________

A) ______________________________

B) ______________________________

A) ______________________________

B) ______________________________

A) ______________________________

B) ______________________________

Now act out the conversations you wrote with your group members. Remember to involve all group members.

12: b) Write your own conversation (Do you play any ..?)

Write a conversation wherein you ask someone if s/he plays any musical instruments, then act it out with your group.

A) ______________________________

B) ______________________________

A) ______________________________

B) ______________________________

A) ______________________________

B) ______________________________

"Do you play any musical instruments? What instrument do you play?"

12: c) Do you like ZPJ?

Write a conversation wherein you ask someone if s/he likes a certain singer or band.

____

____

____

____

____

____

13) Puzzle

Use the sentences found in Unit 8 to help you complete the following puzzle.

After you have completed the puzzle, check the 'Puzzle Solutions' section at the back of the book for the solution to the above puzzle.

Across

3) Do you listen to _______ music?
5) Can you ________ the guitar well?
6) Acoustic _____________
7) Rock ___________
8) Have you ___________ of ZPJ?
9) There is a large _____________ of music here.
11) I'll ________ it a go.
12) Don't you _________ reggae music?

Down

1) I am in a Rock & Roll ________.
2) I can only play this ________.
4) Can you play a musical _____________?
5) Do you ______________ live?
10) Will you ____________ me?
13) Let's _________ you play.

BUSINESS NAME

Unit 9

Sports & Leisure

Grammar Content

- 'I'd much rather...' Phrase
- 'Kind of' Phrase
- Adjectives
- The Conjunction 'When'

Unit breakdown:

In the Swimming p. 72

Sailing is Amazing p. 73

Idiomatic Expressions p. 74

Snorkeling Fun p. 75

Comprehension Activities p. 76

Review Activities p. 77

Puzzle p. 78

What I Like Doing In My Free Time

This unit focuses on …

- Recreation related terms
- Having conversations about recreational activities
- Useful idiomatic expressions
- Expressing likes and dislikes using adjectives

The Pool At The Hotel

1) In The Swimming Pool

A) It's a really nice day for a swim.
B) Go to the sea then.

A) I'd much rather go to a pool.
B) There is a pool here at the hotel.

A) Is the water in the pool cold?
B) Not at all. It's actually quite nice.

A) Good. Would you like to come?
B) I'm kind of busy right now.

actually quite nice = really nice

Now practice the above conversation within your group. Use your own scenarios and say them out loud in English. Don't forget to involve all group members.

"I love swimming under water."

2) Swimming Under Water

A) Watch me swim under water.
B) OK. I'm watching.
A) I can stay under for 2 minutes.
B) I don't believe it.
A) Just watch.
B) All right.

....

B) Good job. I didn't think you could do it.
A) Yes, I know.
B) Here! Let me try.
A) I'd like to see that.
B) Watch then.

Now practice the above conversation within your group. Use your own scenarios and say them out loud in English. Don't forget to include all group members.

---

3) Listen to The Conversation T1

- I can't swim, so I can't go snorkeling.
- Then put on a life jacket.
- I don't have one.
- Here. Why don't you use mine? I have two.

4) Sailing is my passion T2

A) Sailing is my passion.

B) Lester. I thought surfing was your passion.

A) No Pat. I'd much rather spend my time sailing.

B) Do you have your own sailboat?

A) Yes. It's not very big though.

B) Still. It's nice to own your own boat.

A) Yes, I suppose so.

B) You bet.

Now practice the above conversation within your group. Use your own scenarios and say them out loud in English. Don't forget to involve all group members.

5) Comprehension Activity

		True	False
1)	Lester's passion is surfing.	□	□
2)	Lester's passion is sailing.	□	□
3)	Pat owns his own sailboat.	□	□
4)	Lester owns his own sailboat.	□	□
5)	Lester owns a very big sailboat.	□	□
6)	Lester's sailboat is not very big.	□	□

6) In the Deep Blue

Q Sailing on the ocean is quite amazing.

A Is it really?

Q Yes. You should try it sometime.

A I am really scared of water though.

Q It's safe if you wear a life jacket.

A It still scares me.

Now practice the above conversation within your group. Use your own scenarios and say them out loud in English. Don't forget to involve all group members.

7) Leisure Activity Terms and Random Phrases

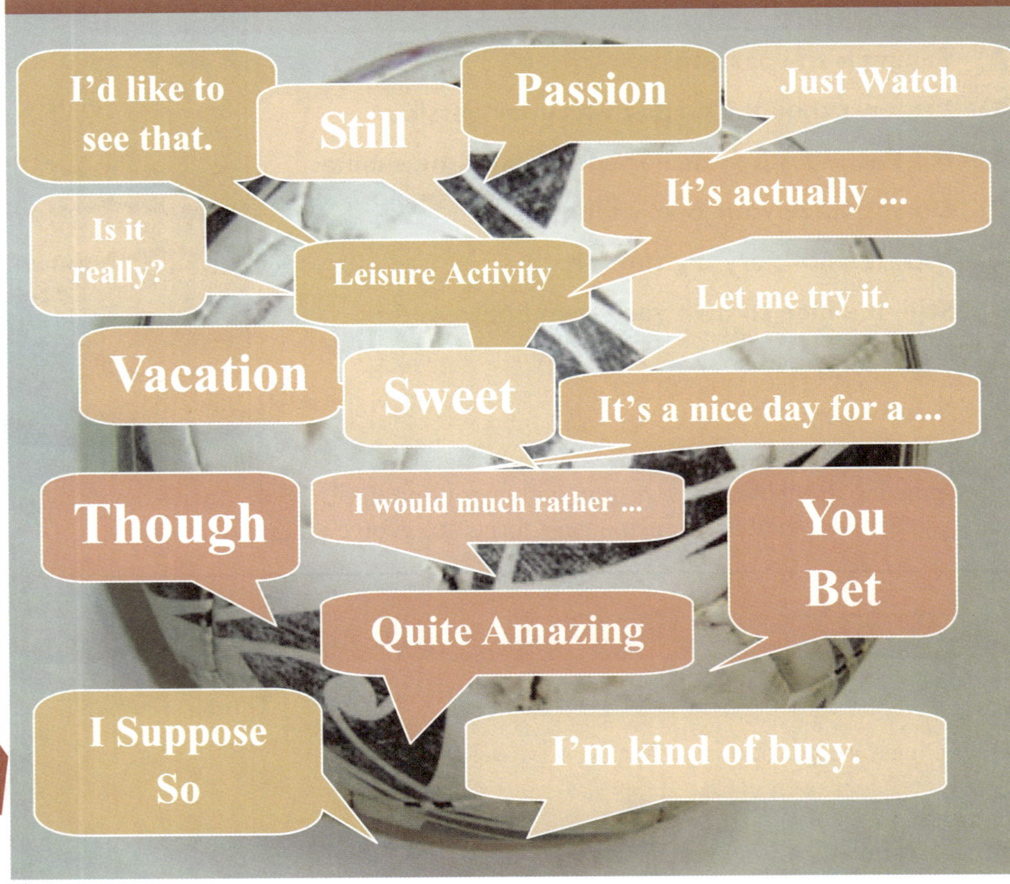

Now practice the above illustrated terms and phrases. It is important that you know how to use and understand all of them. Don't forget to involve all group members.

8: a) Parasurfing is fabulous. T3

A) Parasurfing is fabulous.

B) Do you really think so?

A) Yes, I feel so free when I'm parasurfing.

B) Is it hard to do?

A) Well, it does take some practice.

B) Could I learn?

A) Yes, but it would take some time.

B) I'd like to give it a go.

Now practice the above conversation within your group. Use your own scenarios and say them out loud in English. Don't forget to involve all group members.

8: b) Snorkeling Fun T4

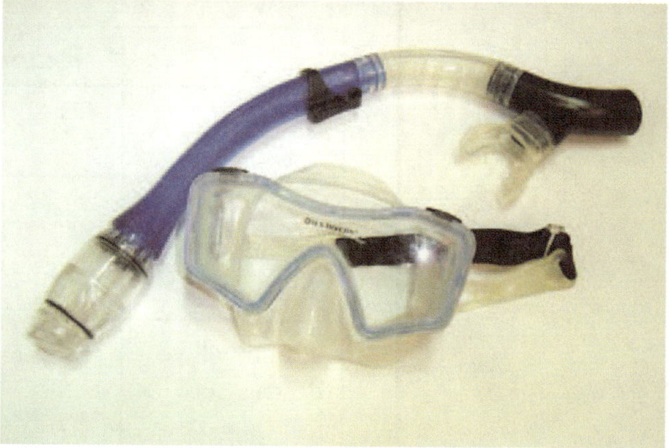

A) I have an extra mask and snorkel. Would you care to join me?

B) You mean snorkeling?

A) Yes. That's what I mean.

B) I can't swim very well.

A) That's not a problem. Just put on a life jacket.

B) Do you have an extra one?

A) Yes, I do, and it's the right size, too.

B) Sweet.

Now ask your group members some questions. Use the conversation in activity 8 as a model for your conversations.

9) Deep Down Below

A) I know it's a little scary, but I like to go free diving.

B) Is that without a scuba tank?

A) Yes. It gives you a lot more freedom.

B) I don't think I'd want to try it.

A) You should. It's fun.

B) No, thanks. It's not for me.

"It gives you a lot more freedom."

Now take the given conversation and model your own conversations on it. Once again use your own scenarios.

10) Fill in the missing information

Can you swim well?	Can you swim well?
Not very well, I'm afraid.	
Do you like snorkelling?	**Do you like snorkelling?**
I never tried, so I don't know.	

Now take turns filling in the missing information by asking your friends some questions.

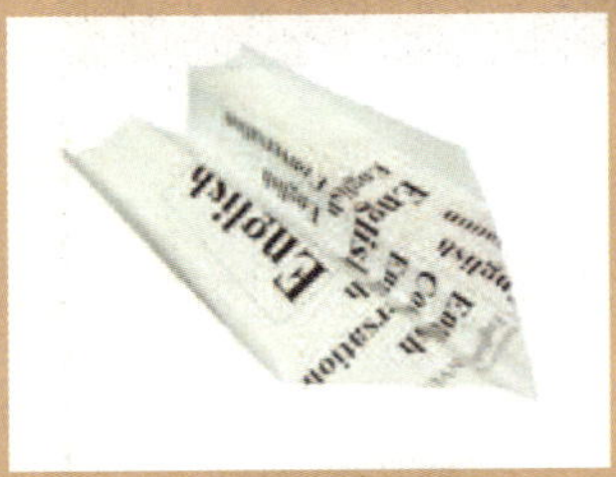

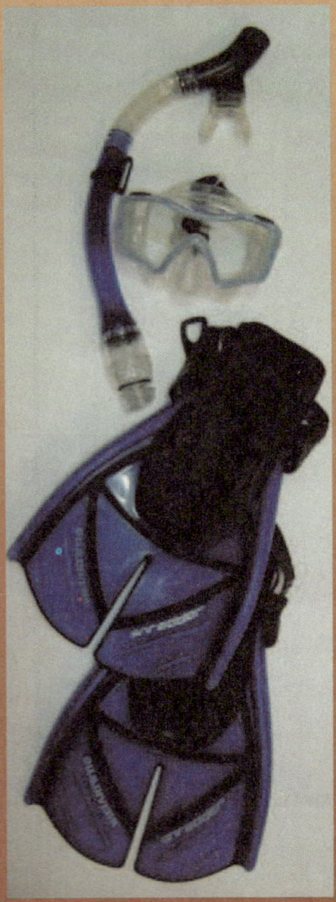

11: a) Fill in the missing information

Fill in the missing information by asking your friends some questions.

	Example	Friend 1	Friend 2	Friend 3
Name	Bonnie			
What leisure activity do you like doing?	I like biking.			
When will you do this activity next?	Tomorrow morning.			
Do you usually do this activity alone?	I bike with a friend.			
Will you ever stop doing this activity?	Only when I get too old.			

A) What leisure activity do you like doing the most?
B) I would have to say I love biking the most.

A) Do you usually bike alone or with someone else?
B) I usually bike with my good friend Janet.

11: b) Listening Comprehension T5

Fill in the missing information by listening to the conversations.

	Lauren	Betsy
What kind of leisure activity does she like to do?		
When does she plan on doing this activity next?		
Does she usually do this activity alone or with someone?		

12: a) Write your own conversation (What activity do you..?)

Write a conversation wherein you ask a friend about a leisure activity s/he is really passionate about. Ask questions as to why s/he feels passionate about this activity.

A) ______________________________

B) ______________________________

A) ______________________________

B) ______________________________

A) ______________________________

B) ______________________________

A) ______________________________

B) ______________________________

Now act out the conversations you wrote with your group members. Remember to involve all group members.

12: b) Write your own conversation (What leisure activity...?)

Write a conversation wherein you ask someone what leisure activity s/he likes doing in her/his free time and who s/he usually does it with.

"What kind of leisure activity do you prefer to do in your free time?"

A) ______________________________

B) ______________________________

A) ______________________________

B) ______________________________

A) ______________________________

B) ______________________________

A) ______________________________

12: c) Casual Discussion

Write a conversation wherein you ask someone what leisure activities s/he's done in her/his lifetime.

____

____

____

____

____

____

____

13) Puzzle

Use the sentences found in Unit 9 to help you complete the following puzzle.

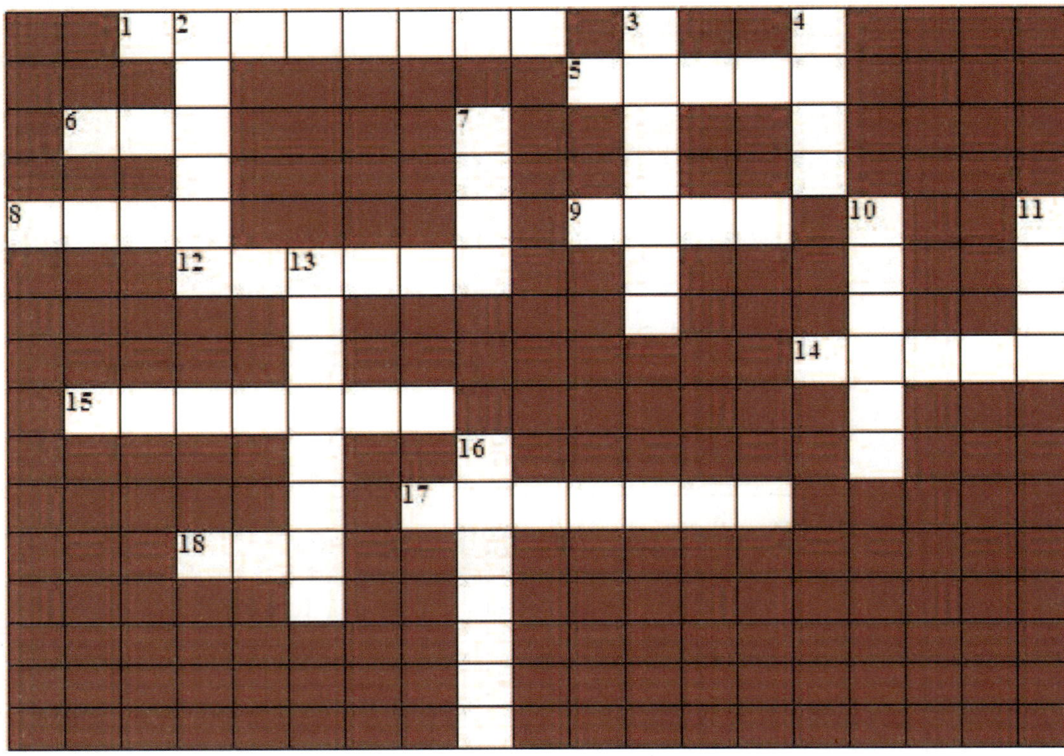

After you have completed the puzzle, check the 'Puzzle Solutions' section at the back of the book for the solution to the above puzzle.

Across

1) It does take some ______________.
5) Just __________.
6) _____ at all.
8) It's a really _________ day for a swim.
9) I'm ________ of busy right now.
12) Is it ___________?
14) Sailing is __________ amazing.
15) It's really ___________.
17) That's not a ______________.
18) You _______.

Down

2) I'd much _________ play tennis.
3) My ___________ is surfing.
4) I'd like to see ________.
7) I'm kind of _________.
10) I'm really scared of water __________.
11) I'll ________ it a go.
13) Leisure ____________.
16) It gives me a lot of _____________.

Unit 10

Into The Future

Grammar

Content

- 'When I …, I'll …' Phrase
- Future Conditionals

Unit breakdown:

At The Hair Salon p. 80

I'll be a Truck Driver p. 81

Future Conditionals p. 82

I'm going Shopping p. 83

Comprehension Activities p. 84

Review Activities p. 85

Puzzle p. 86

Things I'm About to Do

This unit focuses on …

- The varieties of future tense
- Future conditionals
- Conversations about future events
- Future tense conversations

Getting A Hair Cut

1) I need a haircut.

A) I really need a haircut.
B) Go get your hair cut then.

A) When I go to the hair salon I'll get it cut and colored.
B) I hope it won't be too short.

A) No. I think I'll just get a trim.
B) That is exactly what you should do.

A) OK then. I'm off to the hair salon.
B) I'll see you later.

won't = will not

Now practice the above conversation within your group. Use your own scenarios and say them out loud in English. Don't forget to involve all group members.

"Blonde is going to look really good on you."

2) I'll be needing a trim and some color.

A) What will you be needing today?
B) I'll be needing a trim and some color.
A) What color are you thinking of?
B) Blonde.
A) Blonde is going to look really good on you.
B) Do you really think so?
A) Oh, yes. Blonde will make you look much younger.
B) OK. I'll go with blonde then.
A) That's a good choice.

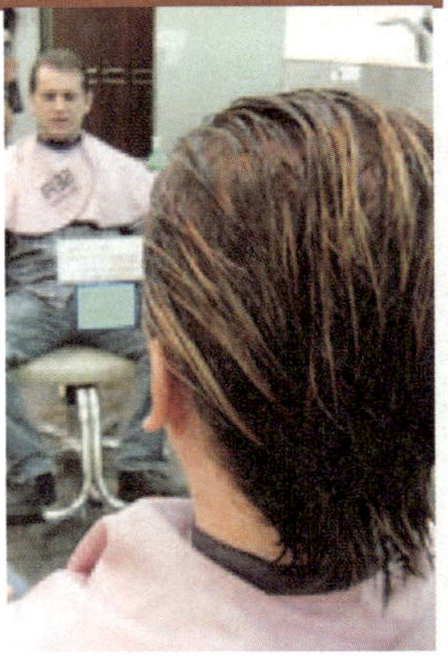

Now practice the above conversation within your group. Use your own scenarios and say them out loud in English. Don't forget to include all group members.

---

3) Listen to The Conversation T1

- After I get my hair cut, I'll look better.
- Yes. I agree.
- I'm going to be more handsome.
- Whatever you say.

4) I'm going to be a truck driver. T2

A) Dad, when I grow up I'm going to be a truck driver.

B) Son, don't you want to be a doctor?

A) No. I like trucks very much.

B) You won't earn much money though.

A) That's ok. I'll travel all around Korea.

B) Are you sure you'll be a truck driver?

A) Yes, I am. I'm going to be one for sure.

B) All right then.

Now practice the above conversation within your group. Use your own scenarios and say them out loud in English. Don't forget to involve all group members.

5) Comprehension Activity

		True	False
1)	The boy says he wants to be a doctor.	☐	☐
2)	The boy says he wants to be a truck driver.	☐	☐
3)	Dad loves the idea of his son becoming a truck driver.	☐	☐
4)	The boy wants to drive trucks to make much money.	☐	☐
5)	The boy doesn't care about making much money.	☐	☐
6)	The boy really loves trucks.	☐	☐

6) I'm going to take the tunnel.

Q **I'm going to take the tunnel today.**

A **Is that a good idea?**

Q **Yes. It'll be rush hour when I'm driving.**

A **Will it be faster if you take the tunnel?**

Q **Yes. It'll be much faster if I do.**

A **I see.**

Now practice the above conversation within your group. Use your own scenarios and say them out loud in English. Don't forget to involve all group members.

7) Future Conditionals ('If' and 'When' Clauses)

Now practice the above illustrated conditionals. It is important that you know how to use and understand all of them. Don't forget to involve all group members.

8: a) Will you take the dog for a walk? T3

A) Will you take Rusty out for a walk?

B) I am kind of busy. Why don't you take her?

A) I'll give you a dollar if you take her.

B) Will you really give me one dollar?

A) Yes, but only if you take her now.

B) OK. I'll do it for a dollar.

A) Thank you dear.

B) You're welcome mom.

Now practice the above conversation within your group. Use your own scenarios and say them out loud in English. Don't forget to involve all group members.

8: b) I'm going shopping. T4

A) I'm going shopping tonight. Are you coming with me?

B) I can't. I am taking care of my children.

A) Why don't you bring them along?

B) You know children. They're so impatient.

A) Bring them along anyway. They'll be fine.

B) I guess you're right.

A) Sure. They'll be happy if you buy them some ice cream.

B) I don't know about that.

Use the conversation in activity 8 as a model for your conversations.

9) Cashing Out

A) Will you be paying with cash?

B) No. I'm paying with my credit card.

A) Will you be needing some shopping bags?

B) No, thank you. I'm using the ones I brought along.

A) OK then. It'll be 56,000 Won.

B) Here is my card.

A) Thank you.

"Will you be needing some shopping bags?"

Now take the given conversation and model your own conversations on it. Once again use your own information.

10) Fill in the missing information

What will you do a year from now?

I'll be attending university.

When will you travel abroad?

I'll be going abroad next Summer.

What will you do a year from now?

When will you travel abroad?

Now take turns filling in the missing information by asking your friends some questions.

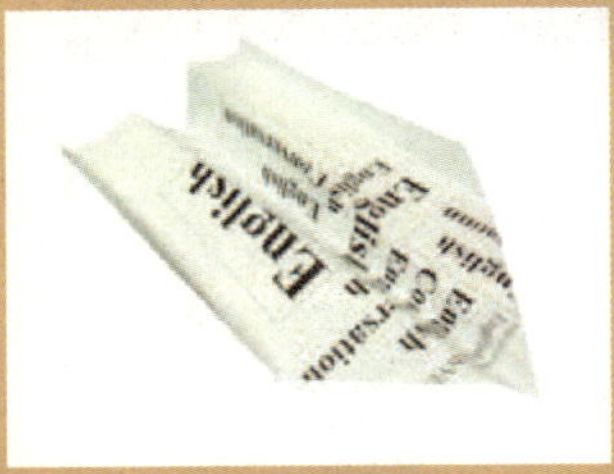

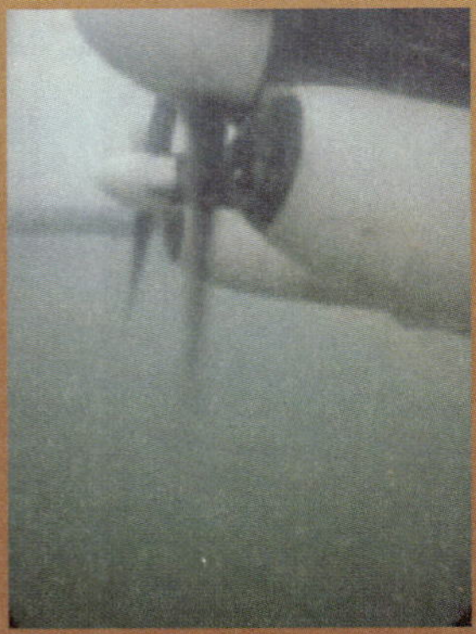

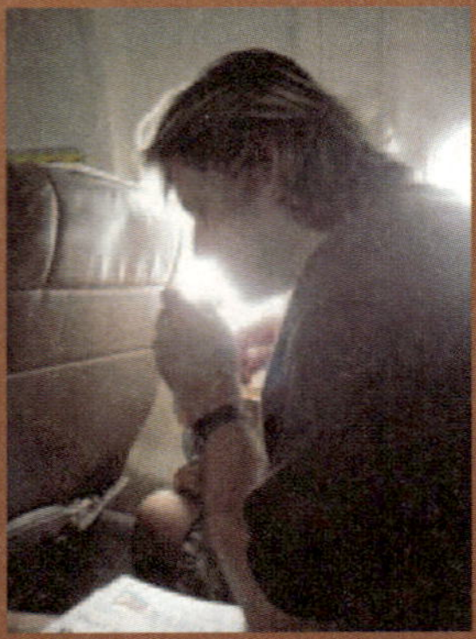

11: a) Fill in the missing information

Fill in the missing information by asking your friends some questions.

	Example	Friend 1	Friend 2
Name	Chris		
What do you think you'll be doing 10 years from now?	I think I'll be a doctor working in a hospital.		
What do you think your friends will be doing 10 years from now?	I think my friend will be married to Joanne.		
What will you do for the next two to three years?	I'll be busy studying at my university.		

11: b) Listening Comprehension T5

Fill in the missing information by listening to the conversations.

	Gerry	Lenny
What will he do in the next little while?		
What will he be doing five years from now?		
What will he be doing ten years from now?		

12: a) Write your own conversation (What do you plan on ..?)

Write a conversation wherein you ask a young child what s/he plans on doing when s/he grows up.

A) ______________________________

B) ______________________________

A) ______________________________

B) ______________________________

A) ______________________________

B) ______________________________

A) ______________________________

B) ______________________________

Now act out the conversations you wrote with your group members. Remember to involve all group members.

12: b) Write your own conversation (What do you think ...?)

Write a conversation wherein you ask someone what s/he'll do in ten years time.

A) ______________________________

B) ______________________________

A) ______________________________

B) ______________________________

A) ______________________________

B) ______________________________

A) ______________________________

B) ______________________________

"What do you think you'll be doing in about ten years?"

12: c) What are your plans for the next few years?

Write a conversation wherein you ask someone what s/he plans on doing for the next few years.

____

____

____

____

____

____

____

____

13) Puzzle

Use the sentences found in Unit 10 to help you complete the following puzzle.

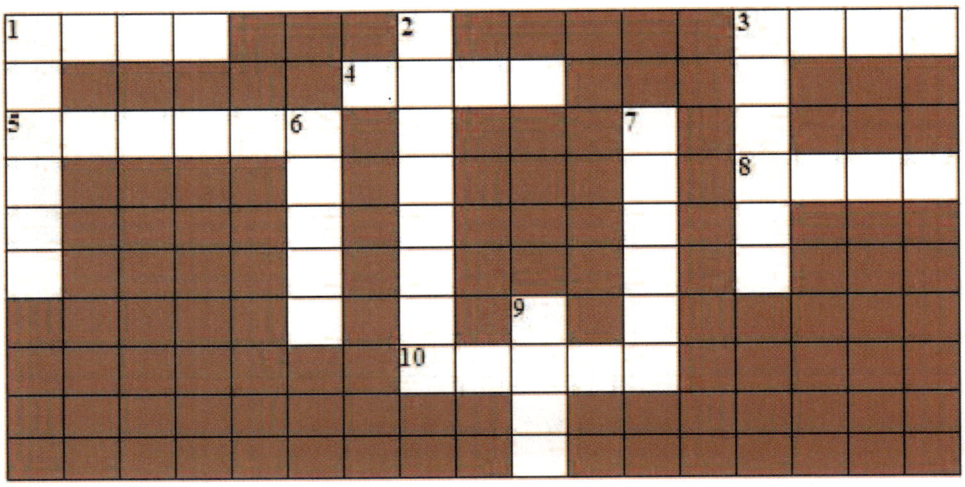

After you have completed the puzzle, check the 'Puzzle Solutions' section at the back of the book for the solution to the above puzzle.

Across

1) I think I'm going to get a ________.
3) What will you do a year _______ now?
4) _______ I grow up I'm going to be a doctor.
5) When will you travel ___________?
8) I'm going to ________ the tunnel today.
10) Blonde is __________ to look good on you.

Down

1) I'll _________ around Korea.
2) What color are you ___________ of?
3) It'll be much _________ if I do.
6) What will you be _________ ten years from now?
7) I'm __________ with my credit card.
9) ________ you take the dog out for a walk?

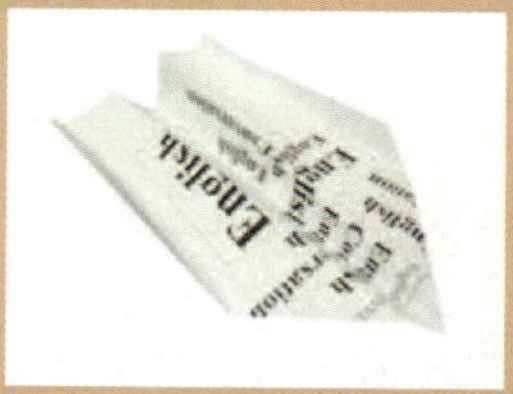

BUSINESS NAME

Unit 11

Long, Long Ago

Grammar

Content

- Past Tenses
- Present Perfect Simple
- Present Perfect Progressive

Unit breakdown:

Present Perfect	**p. 88**
Present Perfect Progressive	**p. 89**
Past Tenses	**p. 90**
When I was a boy	**p. 91**
Comprehensi on Activities	**p. 92**
Review Activities	**p. 93**
Puzzle	**p. 94**

One Hundred Years Ago

This unit focuses on …

- The present perfect simple and the present perfect progressive
- How to talk about things that have existed a long time
- Talking about the distant past
- Past tense (interrogative)

The Moon Is Old

1) The moon is very old.

A) Did you see the moon last night?
B) Yes. It was very beautiful.

A) Wasn't it really bright?
B) Yes, it surely was.

A) The moon must be very old.
B) Yes, it is. It has existed a long time.

A) It has shone for so long.
B) Yes and it gave light to the night.

Now practice the above conversation within your group. Use your own scenarios and say them out loud in English. Don't forget to involve all group members.

"The clouds have existed for a very long time."

2) Clouds that have existed a long time.

A) These clouds are so wonderful.
B) Aren't they?
A) Can you imagine how old clouds really are?
B) They must be very old.
A) They have existed for a long, long time.
B) Do you think God lives up there?
A) If he does, he has lived there a long, long time.
B) He surely has.
A) Let's take some photos of them.
B) Yes, Let's do that.

Now practice the above conversation within your group. Use your own scenarios and say them out loud in English. Don't forget to include all group members.

---

3) Listen to The Conversation T1

- Mountains have existed for many years.
- Do you really think so?
- Of course they have.
- I think you're right. They seem very old.

4) This hotel has been here a very long time. T2

A) **Jerry. This building looks very old.**

B) **Yes, it really does Brian. It has been around for a very long time.**

A) **Has it really?**

B) **Yes. It's been here since my grandmother was born.**

A) **That long?**

B) **Even longer, I think.**

A) **That's unbelievable.**

Now practice the above conversation within your group. Use your own scenarios and say them out loud in English. Don't forget to involve all group members.

5) Comprehension Activity

		True	False
1)	The building was built a long time ago.	□	□
2)	The building has not been around for a long time.	□	□
3)	The building has been around since Jerry's grandmother was born.	□	□
4)	The building has been around longer than Jerry's Grandmother	□	□

6) This barroom looks ancient.

Q **This barroom looks ancient.**

A **Yes, it does, doesn't it?**

Q **I wonder how long it's been here?**

A **I think it's been here since1889.**

Q **That certainly is a long time.**

A **Yes. It most certainly is.**

Now practice the above conversation within your group. Use your own scenarios and say them out loud in English. Don't forget to involve all group members.

Has gone

have arrived

Was going

Were making

Watched

7) The Past Tenses

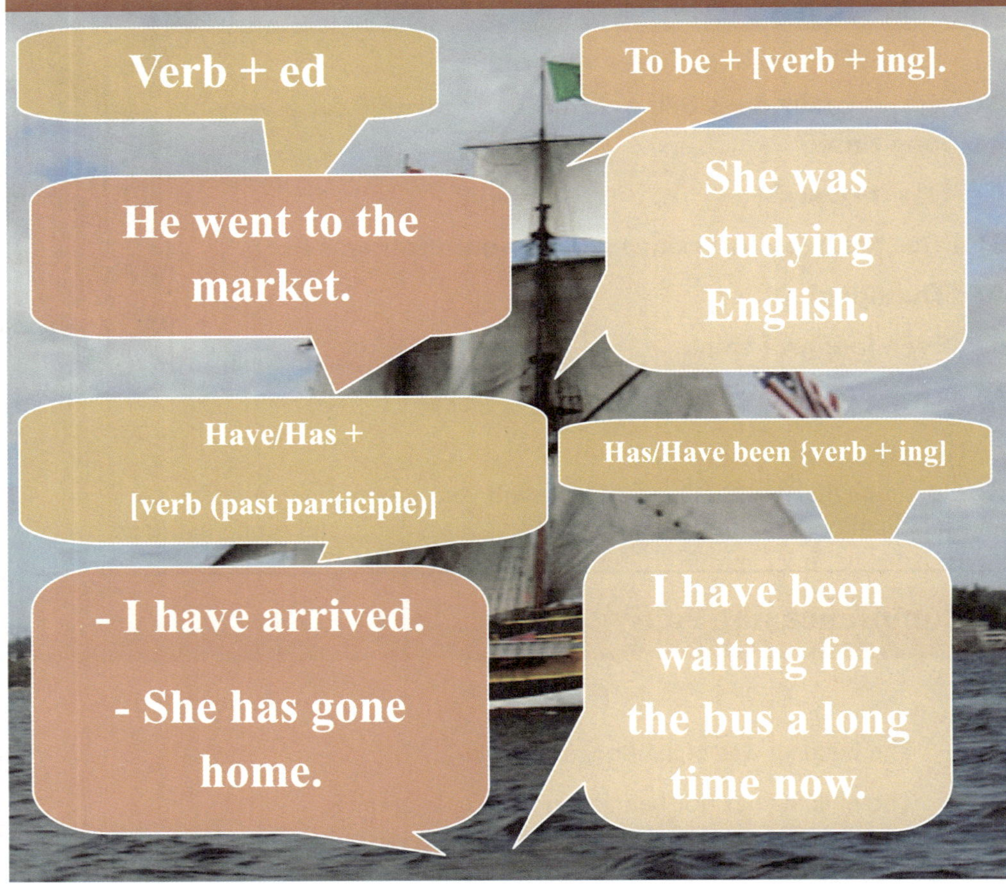

Now practice the above illustrated terms. It is important that you know how to use and understand all of them. Don't forget to involve all group members.

8: a) Tall ships have been around for a long time. T3

A) The tall ships have arrived.

B) I think we should go see them.

A) What are we waiting for then?

B) They sure look like they're from another world.

A) Well, they are from the distant past.

B) They must have been well cared for over the years.

A) The boat washers have done a very good job.

B) I agree.

Now practice the above conversation within your group. Use your own scenarios and say them out loud in English. Don't forget to involve all group members.

8: b) I used to play with my cousin when I was a little boy. T4

A) Who are these boys in this picture?

B) Oh. That was me and my cousin a long time ago.

A) You two looked really adorable.

B) You know, I used to play with my cousin a lot when I was a little boy.

A) Are you two friends now?

B) I never see him any more. He's married with a kid and he lives in Switzerland.

A) It's too bad you two aren't friends now.

B) Yes, It is.

Use the conversation in activity 8 as a model for your conversations.

9) Old Classic Cars

A) This old car is a classic.

B) It's been around for a while.

A) It's from the 1950s isn't it?

B) I think it is.

A) Cars sure looked different then.

B) They are beautiful cars though.

A) I don't think they make cars like this any more.

Now take the given conversation and model your own conversations on it. Once again use your own information.

"This old car is a classic."

10) Fill in the missing information

How long have you been a banker?

I've been a banker for 13 years.

Have you ever been abroad?

No. I have never been abroad.

How long have you been a ________?

Have you ever been abroad?

Now take turns filling in the missing information by asking your friends some questions.

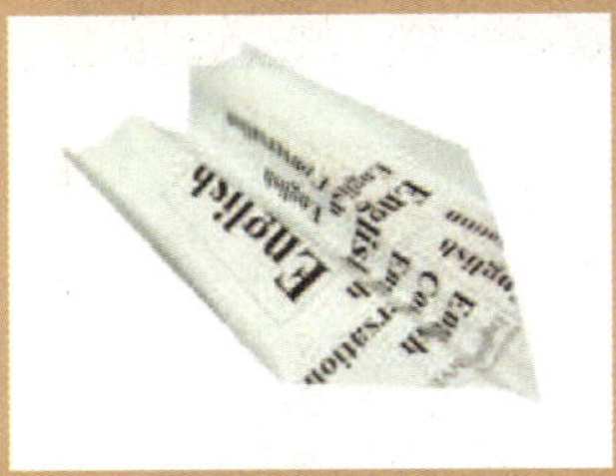

11: a) Fill in the missing information

Fill in the missing information by asking your friends some questions.

	Example	Friend 1	Friend 2
Name	Tommy		
Have you ever been to a hockey game?	Yes, I have. I love going to hockey games.		
What have you done since this morning?	I took a shower and went to work.		
What is the best thing you have ever done?	Going to the Maldives.		

11: b) Listening Comprehension T5

Fill in the missing information by listening to the conversation.

	Terry	Jack
What has he done since this morning?		
Has he ever been abroad?		
What is the best thing he's ever done?		

12: a) Write your own conversation (The ... sure has been ...)

Write a conversation wherein you and a friend have a discussion about a thing that has been around for a long time.

A) ______________________________

B) ______________________________

A) ______________________________

B) ______________________________

A) ______________________________

B) ______________________________

A) ______________________________

B) ______________________________

Now act out the conversations you wrote with your group members. Remember to involve all group members.

12: b) Write your own conversation (What is the best thing..?)

Write a conversation wherein you ask someone what the best thing s/he's ever done is, then act it out with your group.

"What's the best thing you've ever done?"

A) ______________________________

B) ______________________________

A) ______________________________

B) ______________________________

A) ______________________________

B) ______________________________

A) ______________________________

12: c) How long have you been a student?

Write about how long your friends have done what they're doing.

____

____

____

____

____

____

____

13) Puzzle

Use the sentences found in Unit 11 to help you complete the following puzzle.

After you have completed the puzzle, check the 'Puzzle Solutions' section at the back of the book for the solution to the above puzzle.

Across

4) I _____to the market.
5) What is the best thing you've _______ done?
6) How _______ have you been a banker?
7) Can you _________ how old clouds really are?
8) They ______ existed for a long time.
10) _______ you watch the movie last night?
11) What have you done ________ this morning?
12) It was me and my cousin a long _______ ago.

Down

1) Mountains have _________ a long time.
2) I've been _________ for the bus a very long time now.
3) It has ________ here since my grandmother was born.
4) I __________ how long it has been here?
9) The tall ships have _________.

Unit 12

Fashion & Trends

BUSINESS NAME

Grammar Content

- The Modal Verb 'Should'
- The Conjunction 'But'.
- The Modal Verb 'Could'

Unit breakdown:

Footwear	p. 96
Making a Selection	p. 97
Fashion Terms	p. 98
For The Right Occasion	p. 99
Comprehension Activities	p. 100
Review Activities	p. 101
Puzzle	p. 102

The Fashion of Today

This unit focuses on …

- Fashion terms
- The modal Verb 'Should'
- Making a selection
- Picking the right size

Running Shoes

1) Sneakers or Running Shoes

running shoes = sneakers

A) Take a look at these sneakers.
B) You mean the running shoes.

A) They are the same thing you know.
B) To most people.

A) These are sneakers and running shoes.
B) People run in running shoes, don't they?

A) Don't they run in sneakers, too?
B) I guess they do.

Now practice the above conversation within your group. Use your own scenarios and say them out loud in English. Don't forget to involve all group members.

"Those shoes go really well with that cap."

2) Matching Things

A) Those shoes and cap go well together.
B) Do you think they would look good on you?
A) Yes, why not?
B) Don't you think they are too casual?
A) No, they aren't. I'd wear them for school anyways.
B) In that case, go for it.
A) Should I?
B) Get them if you like them.
A) I think I will.

Now practice the above conversation within your group. Use your own scenarios and say them out loud in English. Don't forget to include all group members.

3) Listen to The Conversation T1

- It's hard to make a choice of shoes.
- Just pick the one you really like.
- That's easier said than done. I like them all.
- There's got to be at least one you like best.

4) Selecting a Cardigan T2

A) Which cardigan should I buy, Sandy?

B) Buy the one you like the best, Sophia.

A) I really can't decide. They're all so nice.

B) What's your favorite color then?

A) I really like beige.

B) How about this beige one then?

A) I think you've found the right one.

B) Cool.

Now practice the above conversation within your group. Use your own scenarios and say them out loud in English. Don't forget to involve all group members.

5) Comprehension Activity.

		True	False
1)	Sophia can't pick a cardigan she really likes.	□	□
2)	Sandy can't help Sophia pick the right one.	□	□
3)	Sandy tells Sophia beige is always the right choice.	□	□
4)	Sophia believes the beige cardigan is the right one.	□	□
5)	Beige is Sandy's favorite color.	□	□
6)	Sophia's favorite color is beige.	□	□

6) Tailored Suits

Q None of these suits fit me.

A Then get one tailored.

Q Where can I find a tailor?

A There is one just across the street.

Q Let's go and see the tailor then.

A OK. Let's go.

Now practice the above conversation within your group. Use your own scenarios and say them out loud in English. Don't forget to involve all group members.

7) Fashion Terms

Now practice the above illustrated terms. It is important that you know how to use and understand all of them. Don't forget to involve all group members.

8: a) A Nice Selection of Sweaters T3

A) There is a nice selection of sweaters in this store.

B) I think you should be able to find a really nice one.

A) They all seem so inexpensive.

B) They are all on sale this week.

A) In that case I'll buy two.

B) Which two would you like to buy?

A) I'll need some time to select.

B) Take your time.

Now practice the above conversation within your group. Use your own scenarios and say them out loud in English. Don't forget to involve all group members.

8: b) These dress shoes are the wrong size. T4

A) I really like these dress shoes, but they are the wrong size.

B) What size are your feet?

A) They're size 11.

B) I'll check in the back to see if we have the size you are looking for.

A) Thanks. I really appreciate it.

B) Not a problem. ..... Here you go. Try it on for size.

A) This one fits really nice.

B) Oh good. Will you be buying it then?

A) Yes, I will.

Now ask your group members some questions. Use the conversation in activity 8 as a model for your conversations.

9) A Cap for All Occasions

A) I'd like to buy a cap for all occasions.

B) What about this red one?

A) It's a bit too casual. I need something I can wear for formal occasions as well.

B) Then this striped one would probably work the best.

A) I think you have a good point.

B) Try it on.

"I'd like a cap I could wear for all occasions."

Now take the given conversation and model your own conversations on it. Once again use your own information.

10) Fill in the missing information

What size are your feet?	What size are your feet?
My feet are size 11.	
Do you like wearing matching outfits?	**Do you like wearing matching outfits?**
I never wear matching outfits.	

Now take turns filling in the missing information by asking your friends some questions.

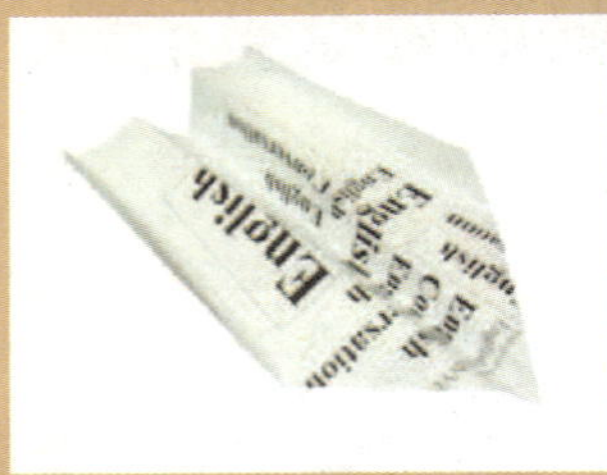

11: a) Fill in the missing information

Fill in the missing information by asking your friends some questions.

	Example	Friend 1	Friend 2
Name	Lucy		
Do you prefer to wear dress shoes or running shoes?	I prefer to wear dress shoes.		
Do you like wearing matching outfits?	Yes, I like wearing matching outfits.		
Is it easy for you to make a selection when you are out shopping for clothes?	It's very difficult for me to make a selection.		

11: b) Listening Comprehension T5

Fill in the missing information by listening to the conversation.

	Flora	Natalia
Does she prefer men who wear suits or blue jeans?		
Does she like wearing matching outfits?		
Is it easy for her to make a selection when shopping?		

12: a) Write your own conversation (Do you prefer to ... or...?)

Write a conversation wherein you ask someone if s/he prefers wearing casual clothes or dressy clothes.

A) ______________________________

B) ______________________________

A) ______________________________

B) ______________________________

A) ______________________________

B) ______________________________

A) ______________________________

B) ______________________________

Now act out the conversations you wrote within your group. Remember to involve all group members.

12: b) Write your own conversation (Which ... would you..?)

Write a conversation wherein someone is trying to make a selection of some item of clothing s/he's going to buy, then act it out with your group.

"Which vest would you like to buy?"

A) ______________________________

B) ______________________________

A) ______________________________

B) ______________________________

A) ______________________________

B) ______________________________

A) ______________________________

12: c) Is it easy for you to choose/select ....?

Write a conversation wherein you ask someone if it's easy for her/him to make a selection when s/he's out shopping?

____

____

____

____

____

____

____

13) Puzzle

Use the sentences found in Unit 12 to help you complete the following puzzle.

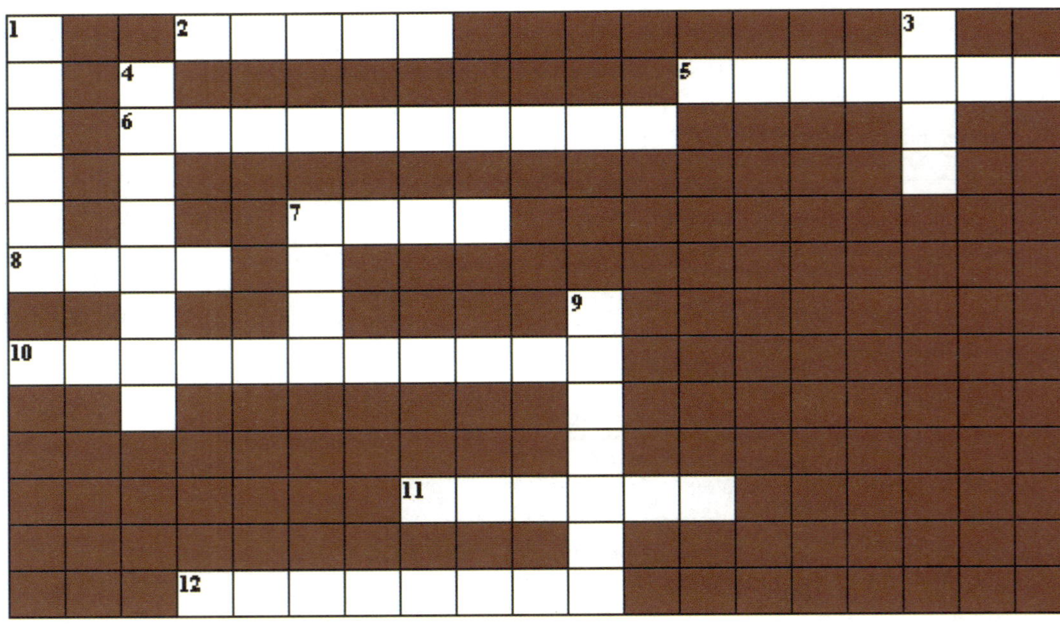

After you have completed the puzzle, check the 'Puzzle Solutions' section at the back of the book for the solution to the above puzzle.

Across

2) There's got to be at ________ one you like best.
5) These are __________ and sneakers.
6) I really ______________ it.
7) What ________ are your feet?
8) Take a _________ at these new sneakers.
10) They all seem so ________________.
11) I really can't ___________.
12) Do you like ___________ outfits?

Down

1) I think they are too __________.
3) Those shoes and cap go _________ together.
4) Get one ______________ for you.
7) They are on __________ this week.
9) Do you like ____________ blue jeans?

Hidden Tape scripts:

Unit 1

T5

A) Hi, there.
B) Hello.
A) Can I ask you a few questions?
B) Yep.
A) May I have your name please?
B) Sure. My name is Jennifer.
A) Jennifer, Could you tell me a little bit about your interests?
B) OK. Well, I enjoy sailing, waterskiing and swimming. All water sports I guess.
A) Yes, it seems like you like the water very much.
B) Oh yes.
A) Now, could you tell me about your passions?
B) All right. I'm passionate about meeting famous people. I'd like to meet Brad Pitt one day. He's very handsome.
A) And how about your goals in life?
B) I want to be a lawyer and earn lots of money some day.
A) That's certainly a good thing. Good luck with that. Thank you very much.
B) Not a problem.

A) Good day, sir.
B) Good day.
A) Do you mind if I ask you a few questions?
B) OK. Go ahead.
A) First of all, I'd like to have your name please.
B) I'm Michael.
A) Good to meet you, Michael.
B) The pleasure is all mine.
A) Michael. Would you mind telling me about your interests?
B) I like biking very much.
A) You mean on a bicycle?
B) No. On a motorbike.
A) That sounds exciting. Also, could you tell me what your passions are?
B) Yes. I am very passionate about being a father to my son David.
A) How old is David?
B) He's 12 years old.
A) One last question. Could you tell me what your goals in life are?
B) That's easy. To provide for my family.
A) OK. That's all, thank you for taking your time to answer my questions.
B) You're welcome.

Unit 2

T5

A) Hello Jack.
B) Hi Marry.
A) Jack, what are you doing during the week?
B) I am going to school.
A) What are you doing on the weekends?
B) I play tennis and I relax in front of the TV.
A) One last question. What are you doing in the evenings?
B) I spend time with my children.

A) Hi Monica.
B) Hello Mary.
A) Do you mind if I ask you a few questions?
B) No, go ahead.
A) What do you do during the week?
B) I work from 9 to 5 from Monday to Friday.
A) What do you do on the weekends?
B) I relax mainly. Nothing much really.
A) How about in the evenings?
B) In the evenings, I play my guitar and drink a glass of wine.

Unit 3

T5

A) Christina. May I ask you some questions?
B) Sure.
A) What do you find interesting about your course?
B) Hmm. My teachers are awesome and my friends at school are great.
A) Christina. How long does it take you to get to school?
B) I live on campus, in the student dormitories, so it only takes me around 5 minutes to get to my classes.
A) So you get to school on foot then?
B) Yes, that's right.
A) Thank you so much Christina.
B) Not a problem.

A) Hi there, Maria.
B) Oh, hello.
A) Maria, I'd like to ask you a few questions. First of all, I'd like to know why you find your job interesting?
B) I would say it's because the work is easy and it pays well.
A) So, the money is good?
B) Oh gosh! It's very good.
A) How long does it usually take you to get to work?
B) Well. I get here at 8 in the morning, and that's during rush hour, so it takes me quite a long time to get here. I'd say it takes around an hour to get here.
A) Do you drive?
B) No, I don't have a car. I take the bus and the subway.
A) OK. Thank you then.
B) You're welcome.

Unit 4

T5

A) Hi, Betty.
B) Hello John.
A) Would you like to come to my apartment for dinner?
B) Sure. When would you like me to visit?
A) How about Sunday at 6 pm?
B) That sounds wonderful. What are you cooking?
A) I'm cooking up some Pan Fried Sausages.
B) That sounds really nice.
A) I'll see you on Sunday then.
B) Yes, I'll see you then.

A) Hi, Tammy. Would you like to have lunch with me on Monday?
B) Sure John. Where would you like to meet?
A) Why don't you come over to my place at noon?
B) Are you cooking?
A) Yes, I am.
B) What are you cooking?
A) Hungarian goulash.
B) Wonderful. I love goulash.
A) I'll see you on Sunday then.
B) Good. I'll see you on Sunday.

Unit 5

T5

A) Serena. How much money would you like to deposit into your account?
B) I'd like to deposit 1,000 dollars.
A) All right. You need to fill out this form then.
B) OK.
A) Would you like to perform any other transactions?
B) Yes. I'd like to transfer some money.
A) How much would you like to transfer?
B) 50 dollars.
A) What is the number of the account you would like to transfer the money into?
B) 123-987-456-246

A) Hi, Gabriella. How may I help you today?
B) I would like to deposit my paycheck.
A) How much is that?
B) It's 670 dollars and 50 cents.
A) OK. Would you like to do any other transaction?
B) Yes. I want to transfer 45 dollars into a friend's bank account.
A) Just a moment. All right. What is your friend's account number?
B) Now, where did I put that piece of paper? Oh! Here it is. Yes, 246-864-835-743.
A) Thank you. Will that be everything?
B) Yes.
A) I'll have the money transferred in just a moment.
B) Thank you.
A) That's all then. Here you are.

Unit 6

T5

A) Hi, Angelina. Where are you going?
B) I am going to the race course.
A) How are you getting there?
B) I'm taking the bus.
A) Does it take long to get there by bus?
B) You only have to transfer once at Central Station and it's only a total of 14 stops.
A) That's not too bad.

A) Hello Kate. Where are you going today?
B) To the market.
A) Are you taking the bus?
B) No. I'm taking the subway.
A) Do you need to transfer?
B) No, and it's only 7 stops.
A) That's nice.

Unit 7

T5

A) Hi, Maggie. Id like to ask you a few questions if you don't mind.
B) No, go ahead.
A) What do you use computers for?
B) I use them to search the internet and to send e-mail.
A) How often do you use computers?
B) Every single day.
A) Do you own a PC?
B) No. I own a laptop.

A) Sally. Could you tell me what you use computers for?
B) I use them to read the news and to download music.
A) How often would you say you use computers?
B) Every other day.
A) Do you have a computer?
B) No, I don't. I just go to the internet café next door.
A) Thank you, Sally.
B) You're welcome.

Unit 8

T5

A) Daniel. Do you play any musical instruments?
B) Yes. I play the electric guitar.
A) Does that mean you're in a band?
B) It sure does.
A) I don't suppose you play rock music do you?
B) No I don't. I play heavy metal.
A) Good on you, Daniel.

A) Hi, Larry. I have just a few questions for you. Do you play any instruments?
B) Yes. I play the piano. I'm quite good at it actually.
A) Are you in any kind of a band?
B) No, I'm not. It would be a little difficult to carry my piano around. I only play the piano at home.
A) Do you play classical music on your piano?
B) Some, but mostly jazz music really. I think jazz music rocks.
A) That's all the questions I have for you Larry. Thank you.
B) Cheers mate.

Unit 9

T5

A) Hi, Lauren. How are you today?
B) Good, thank you, George.
A) Lauren, I'd like to ask you what leisure activity you like doing the most.
B) The most? Mmmm. OK. I would have to say I like swimming.
A) When will you go swimming next?
B) I am going now actually. I am meeting my friends at the pool. We usually swim together.
A) Thank you, Lauren. It was good talking to you.
B) It was good to talk to you too, George. Have a nice day.

A) Betsy. Please tell me what activity you like doing the most in your leisure time.
B) I love playing tennis in the park. It's so nice and quiet in the park you know.
A) When do you plan on playing again?
B) Just after work. I like to play tennis to free my mind.
A) Who do you usually play with?
B) My colleagues.
A) Thank you Betsy. It was really kind of you to answer my questions.
B) Not a problem, George.

Unit 10

T5

A) My good friend, Gerry! Please tell us what your plans are for the next little while.
B) I'll be studying French. I am taking some French classes.
A) Do you know what you'll be doing five years form now?
B) I hope to be working a good job.
A) What about ten years from now? What will you do then?
B) I am really not sure. Perhaps I can tell you in ten years time.
A) Thanks for your time, Gerry.
B) Not a problem.

A) Lenny. Could you tell me what you'll do during your next vacation?
B) Sure. I'm most likely going fishing with friends.
A) Do you have any idea what you'll be doing 5 years from now?
B) Hopefully I'll be finished university and I'll be working for a good company.
A) What will you be doing ten years form now?
B) That's a good question, but I don't have the answer for that one.
A) OK. Thanks.

Unit 11

T5

A) What have you done since this morning, Terry?
B) I've been sleeping all day actually.
A) Did you not go to work today?
B) No. I am really sick today.
A) Have you ever been abroad, Terry?
B) Yes. I've been to China.
A) What is the best thing you've ever done?
B) I'd say going to China and seeing the Great Wall is the best thing I've done.

A) Hello, Jack. Could you tell me what you've done since this morning?
B) Let me see. Hmmm. I brushed my teeth, took a shower, had breakfast and came to school.
A) Have you ever been abroad?
B) No, I haven't. I've never been outside the country.
A) What would you say the best thing you've ever done is?
B) I don't know really. I've done a lot of things that were really good.
A) Thank you, Jack.
B) You're welcome.

Unit 12

T5

A) Hi, Flora. Would you mind if I bothered you with a few basic questions?
B) What kind of questions?
A) Oh. About the kinds of clothes you prefer.
B) All right. Go ahead.
A) Do you prefer men who wear suits or blue jeans?
B) I prefer men who dress nice, so I'd have to say I like men who wear suits.
A) Do you like wearing matching outfits?
B) Sure. They make me look more professional.
A) Would you say it's easy for you to select items of clothing when you're out shopping?
B) Not at all. I find it very difficult.
A) Thanks for your time.
B) Sure.

A) Natalia. Do you prefer men who wear suits or blue jeans?
B) I prefer men who wear jeans.
A) Do you like wearing matching outfits?
B) No. I hate matching things.
A) Is it easy for you to make a decision when selecting an item of clothing?
B) Yes, I think so. I can select something I like pretty easily.
A) OK. That's all. Thank you.
B) Not a problem.

Puzzle Solutions

Unit 1 Puzzle Solution

Across

2) train
5) pleasure
8) license
9) going
10) business
12) time
13) postal
14) interesting
16) passion
17) think

Down

1) usually
3) introduce
4) weekends
6) plans
7) information
11) important
15) chat

Unit 2 Puzzle Solution

Across

1) necessities
3) today
4) for
5) right
7) going
9) Staples
10) course
12) bad
14) awesome
15) problem
16) studying

Down

1) Nothing
2) sorry
6) time
8) glad
11) usually
13) weekends

Unit 3 Puzzle Solution

Across

3) when
4) living
7) think
8) future
9) why
10) money

Down

1) Minister
2) player
3) Would
5) interesting
6) get
9) Why

Unit 4 Puzzle Solution

Across	Down
1) soon	1) start
4) really	2) fabulous
5) making	3) invite
7) tastes	6) Where
9) later	8) should
10) sorry	11) free
12) see	14) know
13) sounds	
15) dinner	

Unit 5 Puzzle Solution

Across	Down
1) break	1) bills
4) pin	2) enough
5) costs	3) withdraw
6) need	8) Card
7) Account	9) deposit
10) transfer	
11) so	
12) banking	

Unit 6 Puzzle Solution

Across	Down
2) possible	1) long
5) than	3) Speed
6) number	4) should
11) hand	7) much
12) tokens	8) that
14) straight	9) fare
15) hour	10) transfer
	13) stops

Unit 7 Puzzle Solution

Across	Down
4) Personal	1) turn
5) print	2) enter
8) often	3) click
10) Drive	6) volume
12) power	7) keyboard
13) plug	9) easier
14) surf	11) adjust

Unit 8 Puzzle Solution

Across	Down
3) live	1) band
5) play	2) bongo
6) Guitar	4) instrument
7) Music	5) perform
8) heard	10) invite
9) selection	13) hear
11) give	
12) like	

Unit 9 Puzzle Solution

Across	Down
1) practice	2) rather
5) watch	3) passion
6) Not	4) that
8) nice	7) busy
9) kind	10) though
12) really	11) give
14) quite	13) Activity
15) amazing	16) freedom
17) problem	
18) bet	

Unit 10 Puzzle Solution

Across	Down
1) trim	1) travel
3) from	2) thinking
4) When	3) faster
5) abroad	6) doing
8) take	7) paying
10) going	9) Will

Unit 11 Puzzle Solution

Across	Down
4) went	1) existed
5) ever	2) waiting
6) long	3) been
7) imagine	4) wonder
8) have	9) arrived
10) Did	
11) since	
12) time	

Unit 12 Puzzle Solution

Across	Down
2) least	1) casual
5) runners	3) well
6) appreciate	4) tailored
7) size	7) sale
8) look	9) wearing
10) inexpensive	
11) decide	
12) matching	

Complementary Activities

A) This is a complementary activity for activity 10) on page 35.

Schedule 2

	Monday	Tuesday	Wednesd ay	Thursda y	Friday	Saturday	Sunday
Morning	Free	Busy	Busy	Free	Busy	Busy	Free
Afternoon	Busy	Free	Busy	Free	Free	Free	Free
Evening	Busy	Busy	Free	Busy	Free	Free	Busy

Supplementary Materials

A) This map is a supplement for activity 8) on page 51.

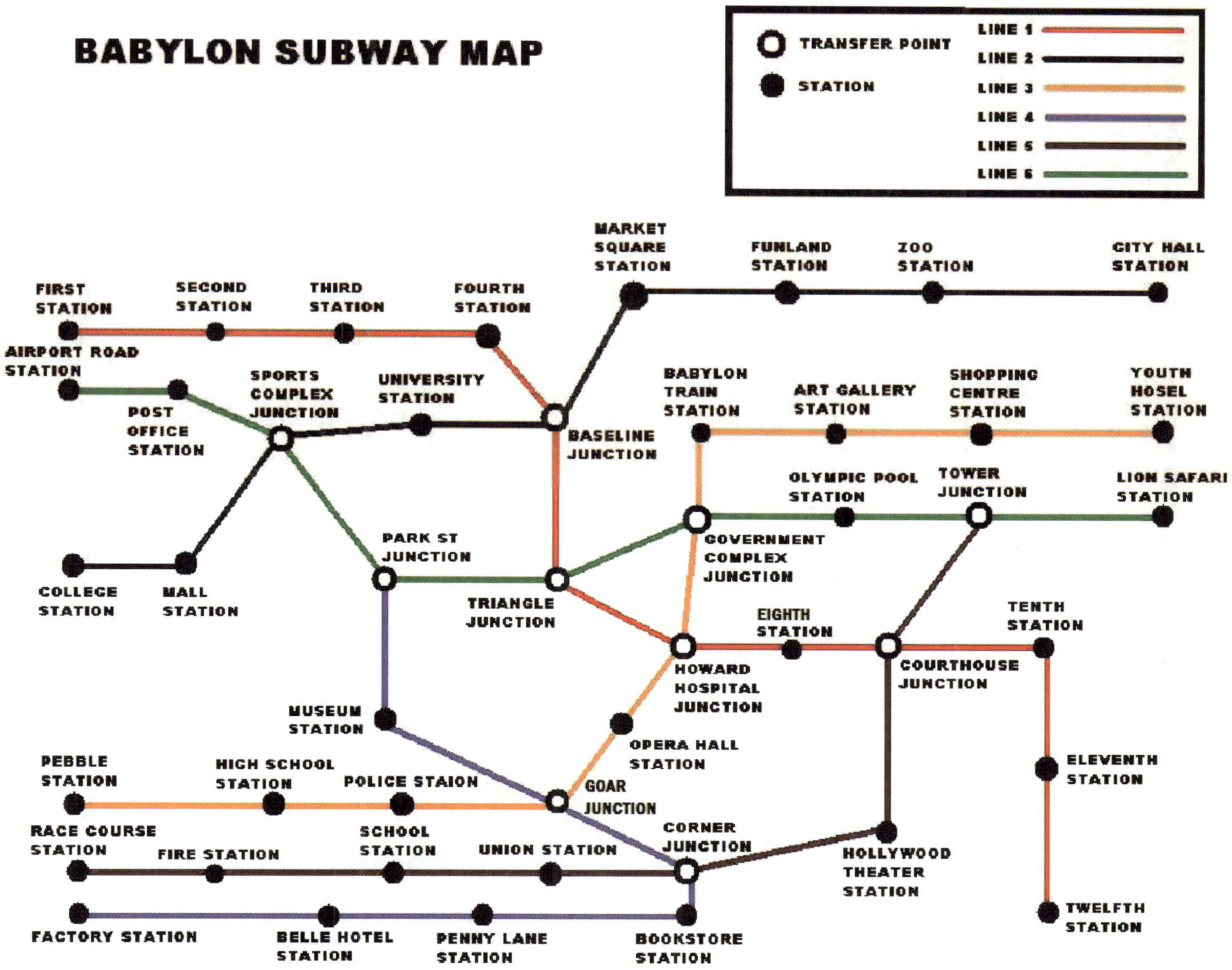

Irregular Verbs

Base Form	Past Simple	Past Participle
be	was/were	been
beat	beat	beaten
become	became	become
begin	began	begun
bend	bent	bent
bet	bet	bet
bite	bit	bitten
blow	blew	blown
break	broke	broken
bring	brought	brought
build	built	built
buy	bought	bought
can	could	could
cast	cast	cast
catch	caught	caught
choose	chose	chosen
come	came	come
cost	cost	cost
cut	cut	cut
do	did	done
dig	dug	dug
draw	drew	drawn
drink	drank	drunk
drive	drove	driven
eat	ate	eaten
fall	fell	fallen
feed	fed	fed
feel	felt	felt
fight	fought	fought
find	found	found
fit	fit	fit
fly	flew	flown
forget	forgot	forgotten
freeze	froze	frozen
get	got	got/gotten
give	gave	given
go	went	gone
grow	grew	grown
hang	hung	hung
have	had	had
hear	heard	heard
hide	hid	hidden
hit	hit	hit
hurt	hurt	hurt
keep	kept	kept

Base Form	Past Simple	Past Participle
know	knew	known
leave	left	left
lend	lent	lent
let	let	let
light	lit	lit
lose	lost	lost
make	made	made
mean	meant	meant
meet	met	met
must	had to	-
pay	paid	paid
put	put	put
read	read	read
ride	rode	ridden
ring	rang	rung
rise	rose	risen
run	ran	run
say	said	said
see	saw	seen
sell	sold	sold
send	sent	sent
set	set	set
shake	shook	shaken
shine	shone	shone
shut	shut	shut
sing	sang	sung
sit	sat	sat
sleep	slept	slept
speak	spoke	spoken
spend	spent	spent
stand	stood	stood
steal	stole	stolen
stick	stuck	stuck
sweep	swept	swept
swim	swam	swum
take	took	taken
teach	taught	taught
tell	told	told
think	thought	thought
throw	threw	thrown
understand	understood	understood
wake	woke	woken
wear	wore	worn
win	won	won
write	wrote	written

Guide to Using Bridgeways.

It is important to realize that all sentence structures can be recycled by substituting certain words or phrases within the structures themselves. The order must be left the same while substituting, for the most part, nouns, noun phrases, verbs and adjectives.

See the following sentence for example:

I like watching television <u>at night</u>.

In the above sentence, the prepositional phrase **'at night'** can be substituted with other prepositional phrases that also depict time.

For example:

I like watching television *in the morning*.

Furthermore, the object **'television'** can be substituted by other nouns that go with the gerund **'watching'**. These verbs would include; news, movies, films documentaries and the likes.

For example:

I like watching *the news* in the morning.

Moreover, the gerund **'watching'** can be switched out as well.

For example:

I like *listening* to the news in the morning.

By substituting the entire non-finite clause **'listening to the news'**, we can begin to describe other types of activities one might find oneself engage in.

For example:

I like *playing tennis* in the morning.

Even the transitive verb **'like'** can be substituted.

For example:

I *hate* playing tennis in the morning.

And lastly, the subject 'I' can be substituted with other pronouns.

For example:

***She* hates playing tennis in the morning.**

Of course, in the case of the above sentence, one must not forget to conjugate the verb **'hate'** by attaching the **'s'** to the end; **'hates'**.

All in all, substitution charts make the process of substitution relatively easy since the grammatical elements that can be substituted are already isolated for the learner.

For example:

I	like	watching	television	at night.
	love	listening to	music	in the morning.
She	hates	playing	tennis	during the day.
We	prefer	learning	English	using substitution charts.

In the first level of the Bridgeways series, the use of substitution charts is prevalent, however in the following levels (Bridgeways 2 & 3) the use of substitution charts is limited, since learners at these levels are expected to rely less on substitution charts for support. Although, level 2 of the Bridgeways series does provide learners with some degree of support via substitution charts, they are phased out in later units, although underlined sections do, at times, bring to the attention of learners that they are interchangeable parts of sentences that can and should be substituted. In essence, learners will not have such support in real life, therefore, it is essential that such support mechanisms are avoided all together at more advanced levels.

Consider the following conversation as an example.

A) Excuse me. What's your name?

B) My name is Diane Southerland.

A) Is Southerland your last name?

B) Yes, it is.

A) Can you spell that for me?

B) S-O-U-T-H-E-R-L-A-N-D

A) Thank you. Now, can I have your phone number please?

B) Yes, it's 0-1-2-4-5-6-7-8-9-0.

A) Thank you Diane.

B) You are most welcome.

See how certain elements of the entire conversation can be substituted in the following example.

A) Excuse me. What's your name?

B) My name is ***Tom Bullock.***

A) Is ***Bullock*** your last name?

B) Yes, it is.

A) Can you spell that for me?

B) ***B-U-L-L-O-C-K***

A) Thank you. Now, can I have your phone number please?

B) Yes, it's ***3-4-8-7-2-9-7-1-0-5.***

A) Thank you ***Tom***.

B) You are most welcome.

In the example below, other elements of the original example conversation are substituted to provide learners with yet another variation of the same conversation.

A) Excuse me **Peter**. What's your ***address***?

B) My ***address*** is ***27 Wellington Drive, Denver, Colorado***.

A) Is ***Denver*** your ***home state***?

B) Yes, it is.

A) Can you spell that for me?

B) ***D-E-N-V-E-R***

A) Thank you. Now, can I have your ***student number*** please?

B) Yes, it's ***756-789-365-234.***

A) Thank you **Peter.**

B) You are most welcome.

Attention, Teachers!

The method of teaching English conversation, encapsulated by the Bridgeways series, has provided the author's learners with great success in improving their English conversation skills. After all, practice makes perfect, and this book provides ample opportunities for learners to put the English language to active conversational practice within the EFL classroom. It is this ample opportunity which promotes learners to acquire the spoken language skills necessary to hold everyday conversations via the English language.

More importantly, learners find the Bridgeways series interesting and fun. Nonetheless, teacher should always keep in mind that the group settings, of 4 to 5 individuals, the learners are placed in have the most effect if learners choose their own groups. It is important that learners do so since they become less hesitant in generating English conversation if they are grouped together with other learners they feel most comfortable with. It is best, however, to place at least one more capable learner in each of the groups if possible. It is left to the teacher's discretion as to how s/he deliberates on which learners are more capable than the others. Overall, the more capable learners have much to pass on to the less capable ones and often take the roles of motivators thus placing much of the onus of learning and acquiring into the learners' hands.

Within all EFL courses, teachers have a duty in guiding learners through the learning process. Without the careful guidance of the teacher, the journey to enlightenment is a daunting task for even the most able learner. It is this kind of guidance which is expected of all teachers ,using the Bridgeways series, in teaching English conversation.

It is essential that teachers go over the 'Guide to Using Bridgeways' (p.118) with their students, before starting on Unit 1, since the Bridgeways EFL series becomes most effective, in facilitating classroom dialogue among the learners, if all activities are carried out in the manner in which they've been designed to be carried out in. Therefore, the teacher is charged with the responsibility to walk the learners through the processes of substitution in the illustrated conversations within the Bridgeways books, in order to allow the course to provide learners with the best opportunities to improve their English conversation skills. Of course, learners are expected to acquire the skill of substitution after the teacher has gone over the process and has assisted the learners a number of times, nonetheless, the teacher should, at all times, keep in mind that learners sometimes prefer taking the easy route, and thus it should become the teacher's responsibility to make sure the activities are carried out in the outlined manner on a consistent basis.

Paul Z. Jambor

Paul Z. Jambor has 11 years of experience teaching English as a foreign language in Hungary and Korea combined. He has been a foreign language professor at the university level for 6 years now. He has a Master of Arts in Teaching English as a Second/Foreign Language from the UK. Moreover he has undertaken extensive research in the field of English Language Teaching within the context of a Korean university setting, in order to determine the effectiveness of the 'Group Style' approach in teaching English as a foreign language. Through the course of his research Professor Jambor has come to the conclusion that the most effective way of teaching English conversation in the Korean university setting is to teach it in a group setting wherein students have ample means and opportunities to use the language via verbal practice. This method may seem simple in theory, however it is nevertheless tricky to implement in the foreign language classroom since most ES/FL books are not geared toward oral practice. Subsequently, the aim of this book is to provide a suitable classroom setting that encourages students to take active roles in verbal communication. Overall, this book is specifically designed for oral communication practice in a simple and comprehensive manner, so students do not feel overwhelmed with the challenges and pressures of learning a foreign language. In essence, this book is the very thing learners need for oral communicative development. The teaching approach encapsulated by this book is tried and tested by the author. By and large, the book is really the step in the right direction if the aim is to improve oral communicative competence.